I0849664

FIXING COLLEGE EDUCATION

A New Curriculum for the Twenty-first Century

Fixing College Education

Charles Muscatine

University of Virginia Press
CHARLOTTESVILLE AND LONDON

University of Virginia Press
© 2009 by Charles Muscatine
All rights reserved
Printed in the United States of America on acid-free paper

First published 2009

9 8 7 6 5 4 3 2 1

Library of Congress Cataloging-in-Publication Data
Muscatine, Charles.
   Fixing college education: a new curriculum for the twenty-first
century / Charles Muscatine.
         p.   cm.
   Includes bibliographical references and index.
   ISBN 978-0-8139-2815-9 (cloth: alk. paper) —
ISBN 978-0-8139-2832-6 (e-book: alk. paper)
   1. Universities and colleges—Curricula—United States.
2. Educational change—United States. I. Title.
   LB2361.5.M87 2009
   378.1′990973—dc22

                                          2008052213

To Marlene Griffith

CONTENTS

PREFACE

For most of my long career as a college professor, I have worn two hats. One is that of teacher and scholar, specializing in medieval English and French literature, in the writing of prose nonfiction, and doing a good deal of instruction in freshman reading and composition too. I have lectured on medieval literature to juniors and seniors, conducted seminars for graduate students, supervised doctoral dissertations, and published books and articles on the subject. I have served as a peer reviewer for faculty publications and promotions, and read many thousands of research proposals in all fields for the Guggenheim fellowships.

But I have had another preoccupation as well: the quality of college education itself. I mean by "college" not only freestanding liberal arts colleges but even more urgently the undergraduate colleges within universities, and indeed any college that pretends to care about the education of the student as person and citizen. I led a faculty committee that spent a year studying the situation on my campus after the Free Speech Movement and produced a report entitled *Education at Berkeley.* A decade later I helped found and was director of our Collegiate Seminar Program, a small experimental "college" on campus that for six years tried out a fresh approach to teaching freshmen and sophomores. Chapter 2 tells something about it. Between and since I have read many books on college education, attended many conferences, met many leading educators, and studied many American colleges as visitor and consultant.

Along with a lot of the people who work in colleges and care deeply about student learning, I have felt for a long time that something is very wrong with American higher education. To people who study colleges professionally, the need to remake the present system is obvious. One of the leading journals in the field is named *Change*. The last decade, indeed, has produced a pile of books on the subject; and in response to the badness of the situation—at the outer boundaries of the education establishment—some new programs and a very few genuinely new institutions have arisen. Perhaps the time for their "new" ideas has finally come around. This book is partly an attempt to summarize and re-present those ideas.

With this kind of life history, I hardly have space here to thank all those who have helped and instructed me. But I do wish to acknowledge illuminating meetings with a group of distinguished University of California colleagues—including Edward A. Alpers, Alexander and Helen S. Astin, K. Patricia Cross, Helene Moglen, and the late John A. Moore—to bring together ideas for the design of a new campus. Those ideas, while they were not adopted by the university, have nevertheless deeply influenced the present work. I am indebted to Paul Christianson, Marie Eaton, Donna Engelmann, Thomas M. Falkner, Patrick J. Hill, Georgine Loacker, Ronald Riggins, and Barbara Leigh Smith for documents, interviews, and other courtesies while studying or visiting their campuses. My friends Elena Servi Burgess, Susan Clark, Michaela Grudin, and Martin Friedman kindly read the manuscript and made many useful suggestions. Richard Holway of the University of Virginia Press and the copy editor, Ruth Melville, were invariably helpful, and the press's two anonymous readers could not have been wiser in their advice.

I am finally most grateful to my old friend and literary agent, Bob Lescher, for many favors; to Jean O'Meara for superb editorial assistance; to my late wife, Doris, for her unwavering support; and to the great teacher, spirited collaborator, and dear friend to whom the book is dedicated.

What's Wrong with College

American colleges enjoy a remarkable reputation. In the public mind, compared with such institutions as Congress or corporate America, higher education is near the top. A 2003 poll by the *Chronicle of Higher Education* found that private colleges were second only to the U.S. military in the trust of the people, and two-year public colleges were only slightly lower, just below local police forces. The public has some reservations about affirmative action, about academic tenure and big-time athletics, but 89 percent of parents of college students report being "satisfied" or "highly satisfied" with their children's education, and the students themselves apparently think that they are doing fine.

Many of us are aware that colleges are growing short of funds, and public financial support shows few signs of improvement. And most parents know that college costs too much. Tuition, going up each year, has become a big burden for middle-class families and made it impossible for many students of low income to attend at all. Squeezed by financial pressures and by press ratings, many of our colleges, especially the private ones, have recently entered into an unlovely competition—using market techniques and manipulating enrollment percentages—to attract the "best" students. Since students in poor communities with poorly supported high schools get poorer preparation for college, that has meant, by and large, the wealthier students. College admissions in America are becoming more and more a matter of social class, rather than an opening of opportunity to all.

These weaknesses of support and access seriously threaten the capacity of our colleges to promote a free, educated, and democratic society. But there is terrible irony in the fact that these are not the only or even the most serious defects in the system. Even if our students had open access and full support, everything would depend on what happened once they arrived; and the truth is that *the teaching and learning that go on in our colleges are actually not very good at all.* The main problem of our colleges is poor education.

We cannot blame the public for not knowing. Students themselves, partly influenced by their colleges' almost universal claim to "excellence," are rarely in a position to realize what the true possibilities of their education might be. They assume that this is the way it is and has always been. Parents who have not been to college are reluctant to judge, and those who have refer at best to experience that is thirty years old.

Some of the defects of college education have been researched. For instance, studies have found that barely 11 percent of college seniors are reasonably proficient in writing, only 8 percent in mathematics, and only 6 percent in critical thinking. But there is a lot that cannot be demonstrated objectively because college education is one of the few major activities in our culture that has not yet adopted reliable ways of measuring its own performance. In the parlance of business—all too fitting in the academy these days—college education has no bottom line. Nevertheless, our failure is clear.

Look around and ask yourself whether our nation looks or feels "college educated." I submit that even though a quarter of adult Americans have received bachelor's degrees or higher, and half of high-school graduates now enter some sort of college, our culture does not look as if it is populated or being shaped by individuals "educated" in the best sense. I hardly need point to our prevailing traits: our indiscriminate consumerism and the media entertainment that promotes it, the steady slide of our journalism under commercial monopoly ownership into the same entertainment, our neglect of government in favor of the buying and selling of political influence, our preference for gossip in place of political thought, our worship of celebrity over accomplishment. The list could be much longer. It is enough to contemplate the situation that most of the business leaders who see us only as consumers, most of the members of the advertising industry, most of our journalists and politicians, most of the people who promote, design, and pay for our mass entertainment, are college graduates, so-called educated people whose judgment seems to be that our society is mostly stupid and should be kept that way.

Whatever "college" has done for us thus far, it has not been conspicuously educational. Even the business community, whose interest in education might naturally be expected to be narrow, has been highly critical of what our colleges produce in the way of high-level employees. A spokesman for the National Alliance for Business calls for "an adaptable, skilled and knowledge-rich workforce. The people who work in our businesses are key to American economic progress, which in turn is vital to the well-being of these individuals and their families." But he reports that "serious gaps now exist between the skills possessed by graduates and those required by today's high-performance jobs. The majority of students are severely lacking in flexible skills and attributes such as leadership, teamwork, problem solving, time management, adaptability, analytical thinking, global consciousness, and basic communications, including listening, speaking, reading and writing."

Education in college is failing, in the first place, because our collegiate institutions are not putting their primary energies into teaching and learning. Strictly speaking, many of them are not primarily educational institutions at all. They have already become big commercial establishments, selling research and consultative expertise to business and government in exchange for fees, patents, and big research grants. No one has put this better or more plainly than James Engell and Anthony Dangerfield in *Saving Higher Education in the Age of Money:*

> The fastest-expanding and often strongest motivation in American higher education is now money. While other aims and functions certainly persist, they are increasingly eclipsed by the ultimate goal of wealth accumulation. There are many names for this, revenue streams or revenue enhancement, lifelong earning power, social utility, product testing, preprofessionalism—they are all tied to money. Money, rather than a means, is becoming the chief end of higher education. The rationale to pursue and to practice higher education is now routinely predicated not on learning but on money. With growing frequency, the ends are not cultural values or critical thinking, ethical convictions or intellectual skills. When these goals are pursued, it is often not because they offer multiple uses or relevance but because they might be converted into cash.

Most universities and colleges belong to a vast, traditional, cultural complex devoted in the first place to providing middle-class youth with a four-year transition to adulthood, away from their parents, surrounded by their peers, where the possible rigors of mental instruction and career preparation are amply diluted with active new social experience and the opportunities of sex, stimulants, and the cheering section. Among these attractions, mental development is hardly thought of by some as primary or even characteristic.

Education in college is also failing because even in that part of the institution supposedly devoted to teaching, the curriculum is generally outmoded and inefficient, and undergraduate students are denied a lot of the potential energies of the faculty by the religion of "research." While research is one of the chief glories of our culture and has an inescapable connection to teaching, its enormous prestige in science—not to speak of its commercial rewards—has gradually infected all departments, caused wholesale subversion of the educational process on campus, and bent the priorities of almost all colleges some distance away from a primary commitment to students. Our colleges engage massively in "instruction," but they do not produce much genuine student learning. In considerable part the wrong people are teaching in college, and the wrong thing is being taught to undergraduates and to prospective college teachers in graduate school.

It follows that higher education must be turned back to educating. The typical American college curriculum is largely based on the simple but debatable idea of education as imparting information, subject matter. The student majors in one subject, minors in another, and the faculty usually takes care that in fulfilling "core" or "distribution" or "breadth" requirements the student has had exposure to a range of other subjects. The list of degree requirements rarely concerns what the student is capable (or incapable) of doing with the information. Can the student analyze, evaluate, research, enlarge, challenge, or revise the information? In short, can the student *think* about it? The requirements don't say. What they do say is that the student has been found to *remember* a respectable minimum of the content of a course on the day of the final exam, and has perhaps turned in some writing on the subject.

What else happened to the student during a course is anyone's guess. Almost the only certainty is that the instructor had an inflated notion of it. A U.S. Department of Education study reports that

faculty often state that they are seeking to develop students' ability to analyze, synthesize, and think critically. However, research indicates that faculty do not follow their good intentions when they develop their courses. A formal review and analysis of course syllabi and exams revealed that college faculty do not in reality focus on these advanced skills. . . .

A major factor that affects instructors' abilities to develop students' advanced skills is an overemphasis with

having "students memorize the accepted answers. . . . "
Another reason . . . is that many professors do not know
how to teach these skills.

What really happens in college courses? The range of possibilities is extremely wide. The best case occurs rarely, and mostly at small, well-endowed, private liberal arts colleges. The student is already interested in the subject and well prepared for intellectual activity by (let's imagine) years of breakfast-table discussions with her well-educated parents on issues from the op-ed pages of the *New York Times*. The class is small, twenty or so students, conducted by discussion, and led by a regular member of the faculty who is teaching a subject that he or she is currently thinking about or even wrestling with. The discussion questions come out of the teacher's current intellectual experience. They create occasions for thought, and they require some thinking before a plausible reply can be made. Our ideal student (who is not shy about speaking in class) recognizes the enterprise. Her imagination readily leads her to adopt a mental stance and attitude like her instructor's. She thinks about the material, makes useful contributions to the discussions, and her remarks stimulate other students to further thought. During the term she does studies on special topics, and after close consultation with the instructor, she writes essays analyzing or evaluating the material. The instructor carefully reads the essays for both content and writing style, and annotates and discusses them with the superior understanding of that particular student made possible by the small class size and interactive format. If there is a final exam at all, it consists of essay answers, written outside of class and with time to reflect.

The other extreme, far more prevalent, and typical of instruction in our large public universities, takes place in a lecture course with hundreds of students. It is an introductory or survey course in an academic subject, let's say psychology or biology. The instructor may be a regular professor, and even a senior one, but he could also be a junior professor assigned to the course because, since it is an elementary course in the field, no one else wants to teach it. Or, if the chair of the department is sufficiently nimble, the instructor could even be a stranger—a visiting professor brought in for the purpose—or, now increasingly, even an adjunct who has little status in the department and needs the money.

In this worst (but by no means rare) case, the instructor teaches the fat textbook, enlarging on it here and there but mostly repeating it in other words, which mainly benefits the students who are not necessarily interested in the subject and have not read the assignment, or those, unprepared for intellectual activity, who find the reading difficult. If the instructor has done this course before, he uses last year's notes. It saves time, which he badly needs for his research. Unfortunately, he is not one of those survey course teachers who has a talent for lively lecturing that can make the material interesting, and he is far indeed from being one of those expert lecturer-entertainers whom the students will remember fondly long after they have forgotten the course material itself. He goes through the book, assigns a paper or two, gives some quizzes, two midterm exams and a final—often true/false or multiple choice—and holds some ill-attended office hours. He also manages a stable of graduate students who grade the quizzes, papers, and exams and who each week hold one or two section meetings or "lab" sections in which groups of students are gathered to discuss questions on the textbook and on the lectures.

The graduate-student section leaders are an indispensable feature of the course, and indeed of the university campus. They make large lecture courses possible by relieving the professor of the drudgery of exam reading and of most of his counseling obligations, thus freeing up more time for his research. They make it possible to say to the general public that the department nevertheless provides personal instruction and "small classes," which turn up advantageously in campus statistics on class size. Funds for fellowships being scarce, the poverty of graduate students makes it possible for the university to "support" them in this manner and thus to provide itself with the corps of advanced students without whom its own graduate programs would not exist.

In the best circumstances, the graduate-student assistant or section leader is a naturally gifted young teacher whose dedication to students and disregard for her own career lead to spending the many unpaid extra hours it takes to make the section meeting a source of intellectual development. But here again we need to visualize, not the best, but a worse and more frequent case. Viewed thus, section leaders are hired hands in one of the most exploited areas of American labor. Under the questionable rubric of "teacher training" they are typically put into a situation where they cannot exercise the responsibility and enjoy the satisfaction of having their own courses, but where, poorly supervised and underpaid, they spend time at academic drudgery that will double the number of years it takes them to get a degree. They are taking graduate courses when they can and writing papers in them. What interests them is advanced work toward the Ph.D. and their dissertation projects. Naturally enough, their interest in their survey-course sections is marginal. A goodly number of them are foreign students, attracted by graduate work in America; some of them don't yet pronounce English very well.

What of the hapless undergraduate in this unpromising situation? After taking a series of courses like this, the typical response is cheerless resignation. Whatever ideas, expectations, or desires the student may have started with have been reduced to learning the system and how to deal with it. The name of the game is not learning but memorizing—long enough to come up with the essay, pass the quizzes, pass the exams, and get the right grade. The curriculum becomes a matter, not of pleasure and excitement, but endurance. In 2002 the anthropologist Cathy A. Small enrolled as a freshman at her own midsize public university, an experience she describes in her book *My Freshman Year:* "She found that [students] could be intellectually engaged, but that rather than engaging in political or philosophical discussions, students were more likely to talk about how they pulled off specific assignments, often with a minimum of effort. They saw fitting in to campus culture as crucial, and purely academic or intellectual quests as only tangential to their education. . . . she found a pervasive, if tacit emphasis on conformity and an undercurrent of cynicism." Small wonder that so many students (and their parents) regard the diploma—the piece of paper and nothing else—as the reason for going to college.

The curriculum needs to be redesigned in favor of student learning, and the faculty needs to be reconceived as a body of men and women who are prepared to give the heart of their efforts to that purpose.

A general model for what American college education could and should be requires broad premises, premises that a lot of us can agree on and that justify its enormous cost. Given that these premises are often intertwined, it is certain indeed that any educational plan should entail, if not embrace, a number of different ones. But if one premise must be primary, my choice would be "education for citizenship." Apart from our humanity, it is as citizens that we Americans have most in common. Looking at the history of our two centuries of American democracy, and at the threatened integrity of our Constitution, it is as citizens that we have the most at stake. It is perhaps not too much to say that of all the possible ends of education, the one indispensable end must be the preservation of a free, democratic society.

That said, "education for citizenship" will not turn out to be narrow or doctrinaire but will instead provide a world of possibilities that have in common a secure basis. Because democratic citizenship is free and participatory, it requires both autonomy and responsibility. Education must teach students—citizens, voters, and jurors—how to make good decisions about important issues. It must teach them how to get the best information, think critically about it, exchange ideas intelligibly with their fellows, and come with them to reasoned, pacific conclusions.

Even from this primary set of goals, we could derive a coherent plan for college education. For we can immediately see that, marvelously, educational goals designed to help make good citizens are also in great part admirably designed to fulfill the other almost universally accepted goals of college education, namely, personal development and personal success. Indeed, we are coming to understand that these goals and the ways to reach them are so intertwined that it is no longer useful to make a sharp distinction between learning to enlarge, appreciate, and enjoy one's personal experience, and learning to have a successful career. Any "professional" curriculum can be so designed as to provide a "liberal" education as well.

It will not be surprising that many of the features that emerge from our premise are already familiar. "Critical thinking," "problem orientation," and "collaborative learning," for instance, have been watchwords in educational planning for a long time. The "curriculum for the future," the new design for higher education that I will describe in this book, is in its essential features at least eighty years old. The reason I call it "new" is simply that while most of it has already been thought, and much has been tried, relatively little has actually been accomplished. The great mass of higher education continues to lumber along by its own inertia on a path laid out largely in the late 1800s, increasingly ill adapted to the needs of citizens and increasingly unprofitable to society as a whole. Recent developments impelled by the culture of corporate commerce seem mainly to be heading us for the worse.

If we are ever going to create a thoughtful society, one that will be able to preserve democracy while preserving itself, some such changes, along with matching changes in our secondary schools, have to happen. We may hardly be able to imagine how most of our present colleges will be able to adapt themselves. We can surely expect some ungainly compromises. Nevertheless, we need to construct within each college a hard, firm, irreducible nucleus of truly educational work. Without this, the American university will lose its identity and American culture will lose one of the great contributors to its freedom.

2

An Environment for Learning

Putting students into the center of the curriculum and enabling them as soon as possible to take responsibility for what happens in class means putting to the side a whole host of sentimental and well-loved conceptions of teaching. A curriculum centered on student learning rather than on imparting information changes the environment, changes the idea and the job of teaching, and ultimately changes the kind of people who teach in colleges. Teaching as entertainment or as a dramatic art, and even teaching as "inspiration," may have some effectiveness in conventional classes, but they lose their validity in this environment. As memorable as they may be, "great" teachers still characteristically tell the students what to think, rather than enabling them to do the hard work of thinking for themselves. You can test this by asking yourself what you remember of the "best" professors—the best lecturers, the most inspiring teachers—you had in college. You will surely remember admirable, "unforgettable" characters and great performers. You may retain deep personal admiration for some, for their intellectual brilliance, excellence of character, passionate commitment to learning, or devotion to students. You may even still remember a few striking facts or ideas you learned in lectures. But it is less likely that you will be able to identify those traditionally striking pedagogical occasions with the ones in which you broke through to a sense of your own heightened capacity to think, to investigate, to discuss, to judge, to express yourself. Your best teachers were the ones who created the occasions for you to do it for yourself. Often, you do not realize this until some time and experience have sifted them out for you.

There is of course something to be said for the idea that students can learn by emulation, by imitating the thought processes of their teachers. I suspect that many thinking persons, at least the most imaginative and motivated of them, have learned in this way. The idea is well put forth by T. Kaori Kitao, professor of art history at Swarthmore. In the course of an essay defending electives in liberal education, he writes:

> The student assimilates—almost unconsciously—the way the mind of the teacher works. All students, talented or untalented, learn the way the teacher's mind works, and when they internalize it, they make it their own; when it becomes their own, they curiously forget that it had to be learned. . . . The knowledge you learn about the subject of a course is its nominal benefit. The real substance of learning is something more subtle and complex and profound, which cannot be easily summarized. . . . It has to be experienced, and it is as an experience that it becomes an integral part of the person.

These are wise words, and in the enviable environment of a Swarthmore, they may all be true. But the key condition cannot be the mere taking of a course. There are rare instances in which the student's imaginative power operates regardless or even in spite of the pedagogical situation, but what is required in most cases is that, as Kitao says, students have the right *experience*. In this sense what is crucial is neither the teacher's mental processes nor his or her personality, but the situation in which the student is placed. The "great" teachers in the new curriculum will not be great because they are memorable performers. They will shun the center of the stage and will be suspicious of the pleasures of displaying talent and exercising power. They will feel, as Marshall Spector puts it, that "in a discussion, things are going well when the students are ignoring me." Their skill will be felt gradually and indirectly, in the students' sense of their own growth. Such teachers may well earn undying respect, but it will be earned slowly, and over a longer term.

To bring off the new job of teaching will require widespread faculty acceptance and learning of a new pedagogy that replaces "telling" students with empowering them to think. Ken Bain, who studied the ideas and techniques of those college teachers he judged to be the very best, concludes that they all provide a "natural critical learning experience":

> People tend to learn most effectively (in ways that make a sustained, substantial, and positive influence on the way they act, think, or feel) when

> (1) they are trying to solve problems (intellectual, physical, artistic, practical, or abstract) that they find intriguing, beautiful, or important;

> (2) they are able to do so in a challenging yet supportive environment in which they can feel a sense of control over their own education;

> (3) they can work collaboratively with other learners to grapple with the problems;

> (4) they believe that their work will be considered fairly and honestly; and

> (5) they can try, fail, and receive feedback from expert learners in advance of and separate from any judgment of their efforts.

I know no better example of this pedagogy than that practiced at Evergreen State College in Washington, as described by the late Donald L. Finkel in *Teaching with Your Mouth Shut.* Although Evergreen faculty teach mainly in flexible "programs" that occupy all of a student's time for one or more terms, use multiple teaching devices, and often teach alongside other instructors, many of their devices can be readily used in curricula composed of individual courses.

One of these, indeed, is called the "open-ended seminar," to which students bring their own questions (about some topic or reading), and in which, through conversation and inquiry, they address some of these questions (33). Finkel particularly recommends the use of "great books," such as Dostoevsky's *The Brothers Karamazov* or Homer's *Iliad* or Toni Morrison's *Beloved,* which by themselves generate profound questions—and counsels teachers to "let the book do the talking" to the students. As long as the class has read the book or been well introduced to the topic, the teacher must trust students to be able to formulate their own questions, evaluate their quality, and discuss the best ones. The outcome of the discussion must not be prearranged, the objective being not to "cover" any given amount of material but to create for the students an occasion to come strenuously to terms with it.

As much as possible, the teacher lets the students do the talking to each other. The teacher provides the topic and the reading and, without dominating the discussion, enters it only lightly, at crucial moments, by calling attention to an important comment, adding a question to the students' list, helping with focus and with the group's summary evaluation of the day's work. The class can also involve formal student presentations, small groupings of students for in-class and out-of-class study, and writing assignments.

Another method of getting the teacher out of the middle of the class's inquiry is termed by Finkel the "conceptual workshop." In this case the teacher divides the class into small groups and provides each student with the same carefully constructed worksheet, a set of written questions on the problem. They "work for a fairly long time on a sequence of questions, and then discuss the results of their work with the rest of the students in the class." The teacher "roams from group to group, listening to the discussions, and intervening when her words will advance (and not obstruct!) the activities the worksheet was written to promote" (97).

Both the open-ended seminar and the conceptual workshop are designed ideally for use in problem-oriented courses. Finkel's description of the rationale of such courses deserves extensive quotation:

These courses are defined as an inquiry into a *problem,* and are titled accordingly. Students learn those parts of traditional subjects they can *use* to tackle the problem, and no more. In a course called *Political Ecology* students learn large chunks of economics and biology as they wrestle with the problem of reconciling economic prosperity and environmental protection. In *Health: Individual and Community,* they master parts of biology, psychology, anthropology and sociology in their attempt to discover whether or not there are new ways to conceive of health care.

Such a shift changes everything. To teach such a course the teacher must have a problem—one that will interest students, and that also interests him. Once he has the problem he can then launch the investigation. It is from the investigation, the attempt to solve the problem, that learning will flow. *If the students are interested in the inquiry, then they will want to learn whatever is necessary to pursue that inquiry.* No extrinsic reasons for learning need be offered, no pie in the sky invoked.

If a student is *not* interested in the inquiry, then nothing has been gained by our shift. Teachers are not gods; they cannot create interest out of nothing. They will be wise, then, not to make any specific problem-based course a *required* course. Better to offer a choice and hope from among an array, a student will find at least one course centered on a problem in which she is genuinely interested.

The second best avenue . . . is to try to *awaken* some interest in the inquiry. This is not always possible but also not as hard as it sounds. If the teacher keeps one eye on the nature of the student population and another on the spirit of the times, he can usually forge a connection between actual student interests and the problem that defines the inquiry. It is far easier to create an interest in a problem-centered inquiry than it is to create one in "algebra" or "American History." (55)

Finkel then shows memorably that overtly contemporary questions are by no means necessary by describing a course he taught, In Search of Socrates, in which perennial problems of interpretation, of political, philosophical, and psychological analysis, were based on readings and discussion of many of the dialogues of Plato, along with other ancient Greek and modern sources. Turning the entire enterprise into a group endeavor, he spoke very little in class, but he had much to do: being in the first place fascinated by the problem; proposing the inquiry; selecting the sequence of readings; planning (from a variety of possible configurations) class activities for the week; making writing assignments; helping students with ancillary skills of research, thinking, and writing; evaluating their work (mainly through their essays); and showing the students throughout that, despite his refusal to direct the class sessions, he was himself an engaged participant in the inquiry.

Some of his most brilliant and compelling arguments are about "teaching with your mouth shut." It leads to a psychological situation in which the teacher, while still preserving the *authority* derived from being more learned than the students, can transfer to them the *power* over what happens in class. He points out that the students' initial refusal to accept this power must be tactfully brought to their attention as a symptom of "their own yearning for dependence," "their own desire to be governed by a teacher." "This is," he goes on to say, "a truly liberating discovery, because only by becoming conscious of this desire can they learn to resist acting on it. Once a group of students learns to inhibit those actions that put the teacher back in charge of the discussion, they can begin to learn to take charge of the discussion themselves. At this point they can learn to govern themselves as a group of equal yet different human beings" (125–26). The democratic overtones are not coincidental:

> Inquiry itself is inherently democratic. . . . *Individual*
> inquiry requires a trust that one's own intellectual powers
> can yield sound conclusions. *Collective* inquiry requires
> that same trust in the group's capacity for inquiry, a group

of which he is a part. This trust is inherently democratic. As many have pointed out, the international community of scientists may present the best example we have of an international democratic community. Whatever its flaws and strains, this self-governing community is founded on mutual respect and a faith in no authority other than that of the human mind. A teacher who wished to train independent thinkers, then, will be committed to fostering democratic aims in his classroom. In promoting collective inquiry, he is already promoting democracy. (115–16)

Finkel's approach is in close harmony with the educational philosophy of John Dewey, which holds that students learn, not by being told, but by having experiences and then reflecting on them. The approach tries as much as possible to create an environment in which knowledge, having to be struggled with, is made into a vivid and engaging intellectual experience. Dewey's ideas have long been labeled "progressive" and have been generally misidentified with the host of half-baked and misunderstood versions that earned a bad reputation for "progressive education" in the later twentieth century. His ideas are ripe for a scrupulous, sophisticated revival, as the successful achievement at Evergreen State shows.

This approach is not limited to teaching social science or the humanities. It is equally applicable to teaching of the arts, to which it is perhaps even more adaptable; and the case for both humanizing and liberalizing teaching in engineering in this direction has recently become more and more urgent to the engineering profession itself. This field, situated between science and the practical world and thus in a position to be of increasingly wide service to society, is richly adaptable to undergraduate inquiry. With American engineering enrollments lagging, and a surplus of ordinary engineers with narrow technical training now found worldwide, competition by our schools, it is felt, will depend upon their producing graduates who are more imaginative, more creative, and more broadly oriented toward social concerns. In science and mathematics, "discovery" and problem-based learning have been introduced for some decades. As James M. Bower has it, "There is no more effective means to convey the excitement of science than to let teachers and their students really do science where doing is dependent on involvement in an open-ended, inquiry-based, student-driven exploration of almost any subject." Major grants by the Howard Hughes Medical Institute to twenty science teachers to improve science teaching at research universities have recently generated many moves in this direction.

STRAWBERRY CREEK COLLEGE, 1974–1980

It was the desire to create a fresh environment for learning that in the 1970s led Professor Charles Sellers and me—shortly to be joined by Professor Peter Dale Scott—to start a new lower-division program on the Berkeley campus of the University of California. We called it the Collegiate Seminar Program, but when it was housed in an old, World War II "temporary" building on Strawberry Creek, it quickly became known as Strawberry Creek College. We felt that the campus badly needed refreshment of its curriculum, especially for lower-division students. In the proposal for the program, we made no bones about our view of the educational poverty of the College of Letters and Science, which, we wrote, had "recently abandoned or weakened many of the college-wide requirements (such as breadth requirements and foreign languages, and specific requirements in natural science) which gave the first years of college certain elements in common, a certain coherence, and which reflected educational convictions of another age."

If the old curriculum had lost its validity and the ground had been cleared, we argued, not much had taken its place; not much, at least, in the way of structure and guidance for younger students.

The academic majors were supplying some such structure, mainly in the junior and senior years. But the academic departments rarely held themselves responsible for the student's whole curriculum, and many lower-division students did not have a major, did not even have much notion of what major to prepare for or how to look for one. Most of the undergraduates were left free to roam through the great smorgasbord of thousands of courses with only peer-group gossip and a superficial orientation and advising system to guide them. As at present, too many freshmen's schedules contained nothing but "survey" courses of two or three hundred students affording little or no personal contact with faculty.

We did not offer our program as *the* answer to the problem, but only as one of a hoped-for group of new alternatives; yet our hopes were very high. If successful, our program would show the campus how further steps toward pluralism in styles of learning could be taken; it might even become a model for other campuses in the same condition as Berkeley's. The relatively small size of the program, we always hoped, should not be allowed to obscure the possible scope of its interest. The campus had already in the middle and late sixties experienced and failed to accept the brave experimental program designed by Professor Joseph Tussman. This program had had a required two-year fixed curriculum of classic texts of Greece, England, and America, taught by its entire staff. It had not been attractive to the specialist Berkeley faculty.

The central feature of our program was the small seminar (12 students per teacher), modeled on the graduate seminar in its emphasis on mutual exchange of ideas through group discussions as well as independent research. To show the students from the first the relevance of learning to their own lives, the seminars would be "problem oriented," focusing on the solution of real human problems. Since real life is interdisciplinary, the seminars would use interdisciplinary resources, including team teaching by faculty from different fields. We wanted, of course, to introduce the students to the methods of inquiry, the "stance," the intellectual styles of the various disciplines. But we felt that for this purpose an intimate exposure to real scholars, and to real investigations in small-group settings, provided that the topics were within the student's scope, would work as well as or better than survey courses.

The seminar was to take a lot of the student's time and energy, more than an ordinary campus course would, and it would carry more than ordinary academic credit. This would clear the student's life of some of the hither-and-yon distractions of a schedule of many different courses and make room for sustained concentration and serious work.

Additional dividends of the seminar model would be extensive opportunity for peer-group learning and teaching, and improved personal advising. The seminar teacher would at the same time be an adviser whom the student would see often, know well, and work with on scholarly problems. The teacher/ adviser, enjoying the student's confidence and knowing a good deal about the student's mind and aspirations, would be better qualified than an arbitrarily assigned stranger whom the student seldom saw and didn't know.

We also hoped that the program would attract research faculty to lower-division teaching, first by creating teaching assignments close to their current intellectual interests. We wanted our teachers to teach subjects—problems—at the cutting edge of their attention. Our motto was "Teach your next book, not your last." We also thought that faculty would be favorably disposed toward a program which, aiming from the first day to prepare students to do original investigation, could be thought of as a natural one for Berkeley, beautifully matching the ideals of a great research faculty.

From the beginning, the program operated on "soft" money: for the first three years on campus funds supplemented by grants from the Fund for the Improvement of Post-Secondary Education, at that time headed by Virginia Smith. This small government agency had, and still has, a splendid record of imaginative assistance to colleges; its budget, however, was progressively cut by the second Bush administration.

Six seminars were scheduled for the first quarter; eight or nine was the norm later on. We never had trouble recruiting sufficient faculty for so small a program, though we strenuously avoided nontenured faculty in the interest of their departmental careers. Through winter quarter of 1979, fifteen regular faculty and twenty-six senior graduate associates (advanced to candidacy for the Ph.D.), coming from nineteen different departments, had served in the program. New faculty were most often introduced to the program by team teaching with a veteran. Just under half the seminars were team-taught by a professor and an associate from different departments; the rest were taught solely by faculty members or by associates individually or in teams.

The courses were mainly in the areas of social science and the humanities, for example:

- Formation of the Roles of Men and Women in Western Culture
- Work in the Industrial United States
- Criticism: Judging Quality in Art
- Literature and Social Change
- Utopias
- African World View
- The Politics of Language
- The Entrepreneurial Way of Life in the U.S.
- Film, Literature, and Critical Consciousness

But there was a generous intermixture of science in its philosophical and cultural aspects, in such courses as

- Genes, Culture, and Human Potential
- The Limits of Scientific Decision-Making
- Food Habits: Biology and Culture
- Technology in a Democratic Society
- Science and Human Behavior

Here are descriptions of the lower-division seminars offered in one term:

Robots and Humans. Philosophical and social aspects of current attempts to build intelligent systems using digital computers. Problems of definition of intelligent behavior and of the nature of computers; moral implications of robot building. Review of problems and successes in recent research.

Contraception, Sexuality, and Population Control. Study of contraception, sexuality, and population control from biological, social, and economic perspectives: physiological bases of methods of contraception; impact of contraceptive technology on sexual mores; survey of population trends in developed and underdeveloped countries; strategies for global population control.

Ideas of Human Nature and Self-Realization. Study of different ideas of human nature and their consequences. Readings in major authors from Plato to the present. Examination of "human nature" and the problems of freedom, social organization, historical and personal change, and the meaning of self-realization.

Comparative Revolutions. A comparison of revolutionary movements in France, Russia, Germany, and China. Study of the origins, causes, and social and temporal setting of revolutions; changes in the revolutionary process; consequences for individuals in the society.

A Critique of Mass-Mediated Culture: Cinema and Television. Analysis and comparison of the roles of mass media, especially cinema and television, in modern culture. Study of social, economic, and political functions of media; media as languages and as narrative structures. Student independent study of TV programs and films.

Women, Work, and Society. Economic roles of women in hunting and gathering, horticultural, peasant, and industrial societies. Relations between work and child care, work and status, work and sex typing. Effects of industrialization and foreign influence on women's role and status.

Public vs. Private: Participation and Alienation. A study of the split between public and private life in America, its nature, causes, social and psychological consequences, and the ethical issues (such as privacy vs. participation) it raises. Materials from social studies, literature, and art.

Enrollment at the outset—seventy-three students—barely met our expectations. Strawberry Creek was never designed to be an "honors college"; we never used grades as a criterion for admission, figuring, as we used to say, that "any fool can teach the best students." But the students who did self-select themselves turned out to come from the upper half of the student body. They ranged from Beverly Hills sophisticates—who had always been in special programs and were not about to change now—to shy persons from upstate high schools who were attracted by the prospect of a small community. On a personality inventory they scored above average in "intellectual disposition," "complexity," "autonomy," and "religious orientation."

I note with astonishment in preparing this account that we originally imagined offering some full-time seminars (fifteen units for the student in the quarter system). We also began with the expectation that students in the program would take successive seminars each quarter for two years. But by the time it started, in fall 1974, we had only (and just barely) succeeded in obtaining faculty approval for seminars of ten units. We fought to detach course credit from mere "contact hours" and to link it instead to student work. The seminars met for six hours a week, but the students were expected to do a full two courses worth of work.

By the time the program was a few quarters old, it became clear that the pressure of the surrounding major, college, and campus requirements, to which all Berkeley undergraduates were subject, was going to be a potent deterrent to our recruitment and retention of students. Letters and Science students were generally unwilling to commit a major portion of their time over two years to a special program whose legitimacy had not been established, and in any case the program was too small to offer adequate choice of subjects over six successive terms.

Further, the initial seminars, however demanding, did not

present a sequence increasing in complexity but rather tended to teach the same skills. Students who wished to could profit greatly in terms of these skills by taking a second seminar; about one-third did. But soon the idea of sequential attendance was abandoned in favor of a program of training for beginning students that was of primary benefit even if the student took only one seminar. From then on we poured most of our energy into this enterprise, but we were never able to pry our critics away from the notion that because our original plan had been modified, the program had failed.

Faculty members designed the seminars (occasionally in response to specific student requests), provided initial reading lists, and a preliminary syllabus. As early as possible the conduct of and responsibility for class sessions were shared with the students. The instructor thereafter acted as participant and resource person but ideally did not dominate the discussions. Each member of the seminar took turns to conduct (or rather "facilitate") the meetings. Outside class, the instructor conferred with the students individually on their writing, their class performance, their plans for individual investigation projects, and their understanding of investigative technique. At the end of the term the instructor reviewed the student's work, assigned a course grade, and gave the student a written evaluation of performance.

We considered writing to be the major vehicle and the final test of the student's intellectual and creative progress. We regularly enrolled some students with more than usually serious writing problems, but very little class time was spent on formal writing instruction, and there were no assigned writing texts or exercises. We found that becoming immersed in a problem of intense personal interest, being given ownership of and responsibility for the problem, being given adequate time, and having to share their work with peers gave students remarkable motivation to write clearly and correctly. This was, in fact, a deliberate (and successful) attempt to teach writing "across the curriculum," irrespective of faculty specialties, and without the slavery of a composition staff. "Composition," rarely if ever mentioned, was taught implicitly, albeit unflaggingly. To this end, one of the cardinal principles of the program was that all the teachers be good writers themselves. And they were. The writing of all of them had been carefully examined and voted upon by a joint faculty-student committee before they were invited to join the program. The program respectfully declined the services of more than one amiable and learned full professor who did not meet this standard.

The students wrote a great deal—a minimum of 7,500 words a term. The first assignments were short papers designed to help students interpret assigned readings by exploring their implications, integrating them with personal experience, formulating concepts, and asking questions relevant to the course. They also helped diagnose problems in writing and analytical thinking. Subsequent papers, often short research reports, demanded greater precision in defining problems, called for wider use of university facilities for investigation, and often helped students identify topics they wished to pursue in greater depth. By the fourth or fifth week of the ten-week quarter, each student was expected to come up with a prospectus for a major investigative paper. Research for and preparation of the final paper occupied much of the student's time out of class from then on. Throughout this period, students commonly maintained an ongoing dialogue with one another and their instructors through preparation of annotated bibliographies, outlines, and rough drafts. The last two weeks of the term were usually taken up with the presentation of oral reports, when students received one another's suggestions.

Close to the center of the program's seminar technique was the training students received in the "facilitation" of meetings. In the course of six years the program continuously refined its conception of this art, and Jonathan Harris, a graduate associate from the Department of Geography and a great teacher, wrote a descriptive statement of it that is still the best I have seen. "Even assuming that everyone is prepared and eager to discuss a topic," Harris began, the facilitator nevertheless can make a difference between a discussion that builds upon what each member has thought about and brought in—transforming those individual efforts into a new, deeper, shared understanding of the question—and a discussion that becomes diffused by aimless talk at cross-purposes, lost in peripheral issues, or mired in arguments over unresolvable problems.

The act of facilitation and its being shared as a responsibility among the seminar contributes to the learning process as well. Preparing to facilitate a discussion forces one to grapple with a body of thought, integrating, interpreting, evaluating, and analyzing it in detail. Facilitating gives practice in speaking and in the best sense "teaching." It imparts a sense of mastery over intellectual material, and thus is another means of empowering students to take charge of their educations. Moreover, the shared responsibility for facilitation builds community and democracy among the class. All participants—even those most hesitant to speak—take turns leading discussions and getting to know one another as intellects and human beings.

Needless to say, we particularly prized this activity because in it—in the individual knowledgeably and sympathetically conducting a discussion among peers and leading it to a reasoned and pacific conclusion—we so clearly saw a skill invaluable for the student's future, whether in community, family, or occupation.

In all this, the method of teaching was far more important to the effectiveness of the program than the subjects taught. In working it out over the six years of the program's life, we invariably operated on a principle that has by now been so well-established by educational research as to become an axiom (perhaps *the* axiom) of current higher-education theory. In the admirably simple statement by Alexander W. Astin in *Achieving Educational Excellence:* "Students learn by becoming involved."

I can hardly detail here the many ways in which students became involved. The students' experience in the seminars—

which took two-thirds of their time—was collegial to an extent unusual in regular classes. The intimacy of the seminars and the members' shared interest in a common problem provided a strong background for friendship. Students often went on country outings and ski trips together. Personal concern for others in the class led to personal interest in their work. The warmth this brought added meaning to the student's own work. Even those students who formally took only one seminar widely shared a sense of concern and collective responsibility for the educational objectives of the program as a whole; many became loyal and supportive "alumni." Once a week the entire membership of the program met to discuss problems of mutual interest. Students had important responsibility for formulating policy on such topics as admissions, recruitment of faculty, and uniformity in grading.

The substantial regular communication among the program faculty (in which associates and professors had absolutely equal status), team teaching, the overlapping of periods of service, and of course shared responsibility for the program, indispensable to the development of the teaching method, also generated an unusual degree of affection. The conduct of the teaching staff in turn gave the students an image of collegiality that most of them were happy to emulate. In these senses, despite the changes in its original plans, Strawberry Creek turned out to be a "college" after all.

After three years, the program was evaluated by a team headed by Professor Seymour Mandelbaum of the University of Pennsylvania and including Professor Patricia Graham of Harvard and three eminent members of the Berkeley faculty. Their report was sympathetic, and it made constructive suggestions. At one point, it seemed to be saying "Campus, examine thyself!"

As evaluators of Strawberry Creek, we found ourselves constantly turning to comparative questions about the performance of students and faculty in Letters and Science: What are the objectives of the lower division program(s) in Letters and Science? What do students know at the end of two years of instruction? Are Letters and Science programs cost-effective or merely inexpensive?

It's certainly a mistake to devote major resources to evaluating a tiny program such as Strawberry Creek while leaving the great mass of established instructional practice unexamined. (6–7)

The report recommended that the program be given three additional years of support, and it contained a wise, crucial, though difficult challenge to the program concerning its "intellectual substance":

It would be a shame, and a waste of a valuable opportunity, if in the intellectual closeness of Strawberry, the seminars were treated as isolated entities generated to suit idiosyncratic interests and failing to address one another in a manner which extended student competence. . . . A process of articulating the intellectual goals of the Strawberry curriculum will probably have the valuable side-effect of increasing the attractiveness of the College to a broader range of faculty. (5)

In response to this profound challenge, the program developed and in fall 1976 sponsored an individual major leading to the B.A. degree. It represented our attempt to show how the program's method and principles could be applied to a four-year curriculum. It provided for individual specialization, with increased depth of study through increased complexity of approach. The major consisted of four main elements:

1. Lower-division seminars, offering problem orientation, interdisciplinary subject matter, introduction to methods of research and investigation, and emphasis on writing and on oral reporting.

2. Upper-division seminars, responding to the student's need for a deeper study of the theoretical and historical principles underlying serious work. These were designed to be broad enough to accommodate students who planned different areas

of specialization and could be of various kinds: (a) study of "classical" texts in intellectual theory (e.g., Classics of Social Science, concentrating on basic reading in Marx, Weber, and Freud); (b) courses analyzing cultural-historical moments (e.g., The Year 1200, studying the transition from the Romanesque to the Gothic culture of France as a paradigm for understanding other transitional moments) or a course in cultural stability, or one in the structure of revolutions; (c) courses dealing with theory of literature and the arts; (d) courses dealing with epistemology, or with theory of science or of scientific method (e.g., The Scientific Method and the Study of Human Beings). These courses maintained the same emphasis on investigation and on writing as was characteristic of the first-stage seminars.

3. Specialization. A group of upper-division courses, from any school or college on campus, forming a coherent intellectually justifiable whole.

4. Senior thesis. A substantial, unified piece of work (usually in written form), drawing on the student's whole intellectual experience and integrating the student's specialization studies. It could focus on an academic field or on preparation for a professional field of study, and could provide the student with valid qualifications for employment (e.g., in business, journalism, industry, or government).

Some ten or twelve students enrolled in our major; no doubt the number would have been greater had it not been for the temporary and sometimes embattled appearance of the program. In any case, two-thirds (two students!) of the first graduating class were admitted to top-notch law schools.

After three additional years' support from campus funds, it was time for the campus to make up its mind about regular status, preferably, we thought, as part of the College of Letters and Science. At this point the program was still small, as befitted its budget, but in the final three years there had been a growing surplus of student applicants. In 1979–80 we had been able to admit only 57 percent of those who applied. The Ad Hoc Committee on the Collegiate Seminar Program undertook the difficult task of evaluation. The committee, consisting of three Berkeley professors and one student, made its report in June 1979.

In presenting the program for review, we had stated that "the Program feels like a good one. Student response is extraordinarily positive, and faculty enthusiasm is high. The Program has a character and being of its own. . . . It is no longer an experiment. It represents a valuable repository of knowledge and experience in teaching and learning at Berkeley that should be used to the fullest in a period in which lower division will be more important to the campus than ever before." In particular we felt that the lower-division seminar—even when taken only once—

provides an alternative style of learning, the emphasis on individual responsibility, and on investigative process rather than on subject-matter, that is not available to lower-division students elsewhere on campus. Students characteristically come away from Strawberry seminars with greatly enhanced self-confidence and an improved capacity for academic performance in the courses they will take on the general campus. [A highly disproportionate number of Strawberry students, four, had won Presidential Undergraduate Research Fellowships in 1978–79.] We feel that there exists in our records evidence of the results of this style of learning sufficient to command most serious attention.

We held that, if perpetuated, the program could be valuably employed to pursue, with gradually increasing scale and diversity, the curricular thinking already started. Our students had more writing experience than other lower-division students, more confidence with large projects, and more facility in using the library. They had learned how to define a topic, how to locate primary and secondary sources, and how to outline and draft a research paper. They had been exposed to the idea of accepting responsibility for their own education.

In general, we felt that we had developed one of the most effective methods of teaching writing that any of us had ever heard of. Accordingly, we had carefully preserved for review all student papers and all term-end reports of student and faculty performance, confident that anyone familiar with ordinary lower-division student work who did a responsible survey of this material would come away very much impressed. It turned out, however, that the ad hoc committee was less than impressed. Its key summary findings were as follows:

1. The Collegiate Seminar Program is a collection of heterogeneous seminars with no connection among them. Its clientele has little or no connection with the "college" beyond membership in one or two seminars.

2. The Program no longer resembles the college envisioned in the original Proposal (April 1973), which survives chiefly in the rhetoric of the Program's annual reports. Nevertheless, the seminars have some virtues and functions that we believe should be preserved, if differently organized and administered.

3. The Program is no longer experimental or "innovative." What deserves to survive . . . should be embodied in a program of problem-oriented seminars dealing with topics and issues that cut across disciplinary lines. The majority of its staff should be Teaching Associates, with a small group of regular faculty to provide leadership and continuity . . . and its own budget from Letters and Science sources.

Although we were pleased at their explicit acknowledgment of the accomplishment of the graduate associates, and of the need for interdisciplinary courses, we were very disappointed that the ad hoc committee had failed to find any wider merit in the program. "The content of the seminars varies so widely both in character and quality," they reported, "that no overall judgment can be made about them" (7). The committee apparently did not find in our teaching method, or in the continuity and connectivity of the faculty—without which the method could not have been passed on—or in our distinctive treatment of students, sources of a real coherence that, if preserved and enlarged, could have served the campus well. It would have been readily apparent, we thought, to anyone who had visited our classes and examined the students' work. *However, no member of the committee ever visited one of our classes or examined a single one of our complete collection of term papers written by students.*

Later, in a letter to the university's Committee on Educational Policy, the committee explained that it "had no reason to doubt the program's claims that its emphasis on writing was a major part of its claims to success. To go beyond this and to conduct a serious evaluation of the relative success of this program on writing as compared with that of other programs would have required a very major research effort for which we had neither the time nor the resources."

The committee apparently based a considerable part of its judgment on the disparity—freely acknowledged by the program itself—between the program's original plans of 1973 and its current character. As one member put it in the letter: "We inferred that CSP had failed to become a College, and that, therefore, its seminars could not have achieved whatever success they may have had in virtue of being part of a 'collegiate experience.' Hence, our recommendation that CSP be discontinued."

The same idea was clung to by the Committee on Educational Policy, which reviewed the ad hoc committee's report and found it "flawed," but was still worried "by the small number of students who took courses in the program. 'Fewer than 1% of the students enrolled in the Program took a full six seminars' [quoting the committee's report]. This supports the criticism that there is hardly a continuing closely-knit group of students involved in most of the seminars offered under the aegis of CSP." The Committee on Educational Policy reported itself unable to make any recommendation at all. Thereafter, the Executive Committee of the College of Letters and Science voted not to accept the Collegiate Seminar Program into the college.

Assuming, as I do, that the program had considerable merit, it remains to be asked why it failed to be accepted by the campus. I must admit that I did not try to "sell" the program to the faculty. In a community of scholars, I thought, the evidence would be examined and the program judged for itself. This did not happen. The committee failed conspicuously to make a thorough and original scholarly investigation of the program, blaming its own superficiality on the constraints of time and the fact that the program had changed its original plan. It brought no new thinking to its task, and it backed away from any temptation to compare the program with those on the regular campus. In short, it was typical of university faculties when confronted with serious thinking about change.

There were other probable factors. One was political. The program had been conceived in the wake of the troubles of the Free Speech Movement and the Vietnam War. Professors Sellers, Scott, and I were well known to have been on the liberal side of those issues, and the teaching associates we first recruited were all of similar persuasion. (What conservative graduate students would have volunteered for a radical new experimental program outside their own departments?) Our courses had continually addressed live political issues, with titles like Sexism and Racism; Tropical Agriculture/Temperate Capital; Contraception and Population Control; Colonial and Anti-Colonial Violence; Genes, Culture, and Human Potential, and the like. Politically conservative faculty may well have been hostile on this ground alone, though none of our instructors was ever openly accused of biased or unscholarly presentation.

There was also the matter of funding. Any new program threatens the budgets of the others. The chair of a small department told me that he would oppose Strawberry Creek no matter what we did: "If you get money, we lose it."

And there was another fiscal threat, subtler but deeper. Strawberry was concentrating on lower-division students; there were even full professors teaching small classes of freshmen, the rarest sort of practice on the rest of the campus. What happens to the university's advantage in the apportionment of state funds if it is perceived that lower-division students deserve the same attention and teaching talent that graduate students do? Furthermore, shouldn't the freshmen and sophomores at the rival

California state universities and community colleges have similar support? I never heard this argument overtly expressed, but it was likely present to administrative and fiscal officers, and to what I have come to think of as the "research establishment."

Indeed, one can hardly overlook the settled educational conservatism of Berkeley's research faculty. From its inception, the Collegiate Seminar Program seemed to swim in a sea of generalized hostility. A group of leading scholars we assembled to talk about early plans showed a marked lack of interest. There was much humor at the Faculty Club about Sellers's Market and Scott's Bluff. A senior professor of philosophy actually visited my office to explain, with a straight face, that the creek beside our building had originally been named not Strawberry Creek but Razzberry Creek. At the opening of the first term, a professor of history did make us a gift of fifty dollars for books, but another professor of history, then a dean, used the term "fraud" in response to a question about the program at an orientation meeting before two hundred parents of freshmen.

Throughout its life the program was in conflict, or in a state of uneasy truce, with key academic senate and college committees. We spent a good deal of our energy fighting for permission to offer ten-unit courses, to get credit for courses taught by associates, to have the seminars approved for the reading and composition requirement, and so on.

Our chief difficulties were with the Committee on Courses, which, as everyone knows, is the lead watchdog committee of the faculty. Other committees may have fine ideas (as, for instance, the idea of the Committee on Academic Planning in 1974 that "experimentation and innovation should be encouraged within the lower division"), but the Committee on Courses is always there to make sure that nothing too unconventional happens. Its members are presumably chosen for expertise representing the chief campus disciplines; but they typically do not represent any expertise in thinking about higher education, and they are given no special preparation for it. Their immediate responsibility is to pass on the acceptability of each and every new course, an immense job unless the integrity of the proposing regular department is automatically taken for granted, or vouched for by a member of the committee, which routinely happens.

But the unconventional course proposals of nondepartmental groups do not routinely meet with the same sympathy, not to speak of understanding. Even if understanding on an issue is at last laboriously achieved, the turnover of membership of this large committee sometimes involves exhausting renegotiations. With a generally negative attitude toward educational innovation, the committee, implicitly taking the part of the entire faculty, usually cites its need to protect "the quality of the regular academic program of the Berkeley campus." In the case of our offering of classes for ten quarter units instead of five, to be measured by the amount of demonstrable work done by the student, the committee was in unexplored territory. Indeed, most members of all the campus reviewing committees seemed unwilling to consider any measure of academic credit except "contact hours," the amount of time the student's body is scheduled to be present in class. *No faculty group, to my knowledge, had ever attempted to determine the actual "quality" of the courses in the regular academic program, against which the quality of unconventional courses might be judged.* My guess is that small "double-credit" seminars, with substantial reading, written work, and out-of-class advising—in which attendance was nearly 100 percent and plagiarism virtually impossible—would have been found to uphold the quality of campus offerings very well.

In the course of the intervening years, I have come more and more to the conclusion that faculty preservation of the status quo as regards undergraduate teaching, its hostility to innovation, is plainly the obverse of its prestige, its passionate defense of time and money for research. When you are in the best of all possible worlds, change nothing! Thus research, the greatest intellectual glory of the campus, when raised to a religion, undermines its most profound civic responsibility—education.

Faculty Responsibility to Students

Nothing of value or consequence will happen in a democratically oriented educational system without the collaboration of the faculties. Manifestly, getting them to approve new curricular structures will be especially difficult. Of course there have been lots of faculty reports, but for the most part they have produced only minor tinkering with the undergraduate curriculum. In recent years it has been the education associations and some foundations—not the faculties—that have led in thinking about the curriculum. On the campuses there has been little general confronting of root problems, particularly of the faculty's failure to take responsibility for educating the individual student as a whole.

There are things for which no single member of the faculty is responsible that are nevertheless the responsibility of all; the most important is the curriculum in its total effect on the student. In the century or more in which research expertise has become progressively more important to colleges, the organization of faculties by academic discipline has progressively clouded, concealed, and finally erased the faculty's sense of this responsibility. The faculty's collegial role of educating students to personhood and citizenship has changed to that of training specialists in subject matter. And the process has been attended by a damaging growth of political self-interest, as allegiance to students has given way to allegiance to intellectual disciplines and then to departments, as valid intellectual categories have degenerated into power bases, as educational thinking has given way to departmental power brokerage, to dividing and defending turf. Colleges of teachers have dispersed into collections of individual entrepreneurs who use their campuses mainly as bases for national and international careers in research.

One of the most deceptive features of this process, one that has seemed to validate and almost glorify it, has been the gradual establishment of the departmental major as the dominant feature of the student's education. The major and its majors, along with the department, have seemed in fact to sum up the collegial responsibility. Academic departments compete to hustle students into their majors as soon as possible, leaving the rest to the mercy of a few professional college "advisers" who have at best a superficial acquaintance with students and no prospect of ongoing intellectual contact with them. Provide for "our" majors—recruit, advise, teach, examine, and graduate *them*—and we have discharged *our* responsibility as teachers. Complacent adherence to this withered model of responsibility has kept faculties from looking at basic questions of education for generations.

It is time for faculties to confront the question of the value of academic departments and academic majors for undergraduate students. If we were planning the best possible curriculum for students as citizens or as persons or even as conspicuous successes in their careers, if we could remold the entire curriculum according to our deepest responsibilities, our best hopes, we would probably not come up with a departmental major set in a smorgasbord of "general education" courses. No—we would not be thinking about departments, and not always, even, about courses. Imagining the problems of life in the twenty-first century, the problems of coping with a future more complex and dangerous than any of us has ever faced, we would not come up with anything as abstract, as narrow, as insular, in short as "subject oriented" as an academic major. We would, instead, be thinking of intellectual powers, of experience, the ability to cope, to come to right judgments. It is hard to imagine how specializing early in such abstracted subjects as economics or French or geology or math could be best for a person just setting out to seriously understand his or her world.

It is the responsibility of the faculty to put the full intellectual development of each student at the center of the curriculum. Each student's schedule should provide continuous training in intellectual skills and a progressive grounding in the basic modes of comprehending experience. Each faculty should define for itself what the desirable skills are, but for most purposes it would do well to start with the National Educational Goal that calls for substantially increasing the proportion of college graduates who have "an advanced ability to think critically, communicate effectively, and solve problems." This means reading, speaking, discussion, and writing, and the closely associated skills of interpretation, analysis, inference, and argument. Left to the academic departments, these skills do not necessarily get taught; there must be formal provision made for them in the curriculum.

One approach is simply to institute a series of courses in specific skills—writing, speaking, critical thinking, and the like—and to require students to take all of them. Despite its directness, this approach has pedagogical drawbacks. First, skills taught in a particular locus, as writing widely is at present, and not across the curriculum tend to be regarded by students as subjects to be passed and then forgotten. Second, although skills cannot be taught in the absence of subject matter, they are best taught in connection with subject matter that is of particular interest to students. Third, skills taught as subjects of the course itself run the risk of being *taught about* rather than being learned. In well-designed seminars, skills are learned almost unconsciously in the course of wrestling with interesting problems in the company of peers. For these reasons it is essential that the curriculum embody—take responsibility for—the basic skills and provide direct experience with them. Each course can be planned and evaluated for the skills it teaches. In this light, sensitive advising on the student's course of study becomes crucial, and the student and adviser can be jointly held responsible for the character of the student's total curricular experience.

Provision must also be made for experience of the basic disciplines. Some skills, such as communication and reasoning, are clearly generic and border on being disciplines themselves; they are transferable over a wide range of activities. Nevertheless, sophisticated communication and reasoning require firm orientation in the domain of study involved. Making judgments about a historical situation requires a different stance and different methods than does judging a musical performance, and solving a social problem is similarly different from solving one in physics. The faculty will have to decide what the basic disciplinary modes are, and make sure that the student has experience in them.

We can be certain that the conventional subjects conventionally taught—which usually represent divisions of turf and budget rather than essential disciplines—will not satisfactorily define educational breadth. I still remember with shame, as a young member of a university committee on educational policy, complacently joining the consensus for dividing the "breadth" component of every student's curriculum into equal numbers of required departmental courses in "science," "social science," and "humanities." Neither I nor any other member of this august body had done the slightest study of what this sort of division—or "distribution," as it is widely called—would do for students. But it tacitly made for peace among the departments. Once the departments or the divisions capture their share of the students, they happily teach their subject matter, with little regard for whether their essential disciplinary skills are learned or not.

Opinions differ, of course, as to what the basic disciplines really are, but the conventional formulations seem too crude to be useful. The conventional idea of disciplines derives from the various branches of knowledge, or subject matter, each with its community, and its traditional concepts and language. In this sense, "science" may well be a discipline, but "social science" surely is a combination of several, and the "humanities," however you define it (or them), are even more variegated. A better beginning might be made by trying to distinguish the disciplines less in terms of their objects of study than in terms of the methods involved in that study—logical, empirical, statistical, historical, critical (analytic, evaluative), creative—and making sure that the student gets practice in as many of them as possible.

If the academic departments do not hold themselves responsible for the teaching of basic skills and methods, neither do they reliably provide what is piously but erroneously imagined to be their key justification: study in depth. A typical formulation of the curricular requirement for a major is "in-depth study of at least one academic subject." The academic major subjects may have crucial value in graduate work and in apportioning research—some division of knowledge into categories being inescapable in a rational organization of scholarship—but their domination of the *undergraduate* curriculum represents a deep if unacknowledged fantasy on the part of faculties that the best issue of this curriculum must be reproductions of themselves. Let us grant that undergraduate academic majors provide vocational training for future academics, but an assemblage of courses taken in one department—which is all that many majors amount to—does not necessarily produce depth. According to the Association of American Colleges report *Integrity in the College Curriculum:*

> Study in depth . . . is not so much an additional component of the curriculum as it is recognition of the complexity and sophistication with which the various components are interrelated and understood. . . . depth, we are certain, does not arise merely from the existence of an extensive factual base. For our purposes a course of study has depth if it in fact offers a complex structure of knowledge. The comprehension of this structure—a decent understanding and control of it—is what we mean by study in depth. (28)

Once we realize that simply learning more and more about one subject does not constitute depth, it becomes easier to see that depth is a matter of comprehending complex structures, of understanding the interrelatedness of many factors in a given problem or situation or field. *As such, it is inseparable from breadth.* For instance, once you move from the facts of a given situation to its causes and effects, to its historical and ethical dimensions, and then to its theoretical underpinnings, you are moving toward depth. You are also, manifestly, moving into several other basic disciplines as well. This suggests that from a curricular point of view, breadth and depth should not—probably cannot—be seen and planned for as separable attributes of a student's program but rather are achieved in proportion to the student's capacity to deal with complexity itself.

The traditional academic disciplines offered for study in depth, if they have the requisite complexity, can be justified on that basis alone, as the ultimate intellectual exercise that gives students their first insight into the complexity of knowledge itself. But justified as they may be, they are not the only or even necessarily the best ways to achieve depth. Many of these disciplines have an abstraction and a narrowness that do not recommend them to students who may not contemplate academic careers and who want this central effort in their college careers to lead with clearer relevance to their later lives. For such students, interdisciplinary studies and professional studies offer a powerful alternative, always providing that they offer the requisite complexity (*Integrity* 30).

Interdisciplinary studies naturally tend to be complex because they entail comprehension of a variety of fields of knowledge and of a variety of methods of study. As I shall propose in some detail in chapter 4, a curriculum seen as a graded series of interdisciplinary seminars of increasing complexity, culminating in a large senior project, would provide breadth and depth simultaneously, and could reliably focus the faculty's attention upon the student's actual intellectual achievement. With sensitive advising, such a curriculum would provide each student with a "major" of skills and information much deeper and broader than most colleges envision at present.

Planning such a series, or even determining how to assess a given seminar for complexity, would be a major intellectual challenge, well worthy of a good faculty. Such planning has rarely been done, but would do much to define the true nature of the curriculum for the faculty itself.

Having come down in favor of defining the curriculum in terms of key skills and disciplines, it remains for us to give subject matter its due. As we have repeatedly noted, learning cannot go on without it. But it does not matter what subject is studied as long as it supplies the requisite interest, potential complexity, and contribution to the student's powers. This means that most if not all of the conventional "subjects" of the liberal arts curriculum may be brought into the new curriculum as vehicles for development of the student's cognitive skills.

The choice of subject matter should depend on the student's background, experience, and goals; it should respect individual differences and also be able to challenge those differences. As a veteran teacher of literature, I may be excused for believing that the study of great texts could not be improved upon for this purpose. In addition to the development of the student's power of reading, which is of course applicable to a great range of other life situations, it raises all the profoundest problems of living in a way that is fascinating to students. But no one could deny that any of the other conventional academic subjects—science, math, social science, history, philosophy, art, languages—can yield engrossing, complex problems for study. In later chapters I offer many descriptions of actual courses that specify the problems they address.

A Curriculum Design for the Future

There is now remarkable agreement among educational thinkers about what best promotes student learning. Above all, students learn when they are *engaged* in the process. They respond well to high expectations, prompt feedback, and challenging problems related to their backgrounds, history, and goals. Students flourish in communities, with the support and collaboration of their peers. They develop best when the curriculum is coherent, progressive, and clear in its goals. Their learning is deepened and strengthened when it is active and related to concrete experience. Service-oriented classes and outside work/service programs contribute powerfully to learning how theory relates to practice, and to how using knowledge well depends on dealing with the social and cultural setting of one's work. Student engagement is also deeply stimulated by contact with teachers outside of class and by extracurricular activities. To describe all the features of an ideal college here would be impossible, but one can at least imagine an ideal curriculum that would accommodate the different ways of learning and knowing that students bring with them.

THE NUCLEUS

The undergraduate's education should have as its nucleus a continuous series of small classes that provide the optimum learning environment. I use the nuclear metaphor here deliberately, both to urge the centrality of this activity and also to leave ample, complementary, provision in the curriculum for what I call "planetary" studies: the application of both traditional and new technological means to rounding out the student's knowledge and experience.

Practice suggests that, to give the professor intimate knowledge of each student's character and progress, and enough time for generous conferences, an ideal class not be larger than sixteen or eighteen. However, to ensure a critical mass sufficient for a varied mix of student talents, ideas, and attitudes, it should not be smaller than ten or twelve. This kind of class is commonly called a seminar.

The seminar should always have a definite subject, but its primary object should be training in intellectual skills by means of reading, scholarly investigation, discussion, and writing; and its success should thus be judged by the intellectual *quality* of the work done, rather than by the quantity of specific course material memorized. The teacher should provide the subject of the seminar and the initial reading or other investigative means, should supervise and occasionally join (but generally not lead) the discussions, confer with students individually on writing and general progress, act as their academic adviser, and evaluate their work. The seminar should focus on serious problems of interest to both students and teachers; thus it should often be interdisciplinary and, where the topic requires, team-taught. The reason for this is that most serious problems, like most life experiences, are interdisciplinary.

Interdisciplinary, problem-oriented seminars are thus ideally suited to the purposes of the nuclear part of the curriculum. Year by year the seminars should become increasingly sophisticated, so that with careful and informed advising the student's experience in the major modes of thinking widens. The senior seminar requires a serious, major project drawing on the student's whole intellectual experience. Such projects do not merely summarize the student's undergraduate education but may aim onward, leading toward a vocational goal, providing valid experience for employment (e.g., in business, industry, communications, social service, or government), or toward graduate and professional studies.

A series of seminars can take from a quarter to a third of the student's work time, and since it is aimed at the most widely desired outcomes of undergraduate education—and not at narrow subject-matter specialism—can properly be called the student's "major." This curricular nucleus, conscientiously administered and rigorously evaluated, would represent the faculty's collective responsibility for each student's intellectual development within the college curriculum. As we have seen, this responsibility is at present shamelessly neglected.

It is worth noting that one of the most innovative universities in the world, Aalborg University in Denmark, reports great success with an undergraduate curriculum based heavily on seminars and problem orientation:

> One of Aalborg University's trademarks is its unique pedagogic model of teaching: the problem-based, project-organized model (PBL, Problem-based Learning). With this method a great part of the semester teaching and student work revolves around complex real-life problems or issues that the students wonder about and try to find answers to in scientific manners while working together in groups. A recent evaluation from the Organisation for Economic Co-operation and Development (OECD) has shown that this form of teaching is close to optimal for the learning process.

PLANETARY STUDIES

Traditional academic courses still have a clear, if delimited, value for undergraduates. Students should still be free to explore a wide range of areas that may beckon, whether prompted by previous study or by natural curiosity; and faculties should be free to require certain special subjects as essential information for citizenship. In the design I am describing, then, there is a sphere of studies surrounding the nucleus of seminars, nourishing the latter and extending the range of the student's learning. Faculties could come to offer whole programs in this configuration, with successive seminars offered along with groups of planetary courses that would feed into them.

This broad selection of studies, by virtue of its planetary locus in the student's course of study, takes on a character quite different from that of the nonmajor "electives" common in the ordinary curriculum. Since the nucleus of seminars bears the principal responsibility for the students' exposure to the key intellectual skills and for their intellectual progress, and by its scale and intimacy guarantees the integrity of their performance, it at the same time liberates the faculty in the running and grading of the rest of the courses. In planetary courses it is no longer necessary to be so concerned with calling the roll, or with the class quizzes that so often have the sole function of enforcing attendance. It is no longer necessary for conscientious teachers concerned with the intellectual rigor and pedagogical respectability of larger classes to resort to what usually turn out to be desperate half measures: conducting "discussions" with groups too large for general participation, dividing the class into "discussion sections" led by overworked assistants, assigning term papers too numerous to be read responsibly (or having them read by assistants who are equally unable to read them responsibly), conducting essay-type final examinations for too many students to be evaluated or having the answers read by the same hapless assistants, and worrying about plagiarism on the same papers and examinations.

A strong, continuous nuclear seminar program frees the faculty to plan the other courses at their most economical size—namely, as large as practicable—and thus pays for itself at the same time. Intermediate-sized courses—too large to be efficient seminars, too small to be economical lectures—can be safely discontinued.

Deep and sensitive evaluation of student performance in the seminars makes grading in the rest of the curriculum much simpler. There, where the emphasis is candidly on knowing the subject matter, quantitative measures (true/false, multiple choice, etc.) become more plausible and defensible means of gauging student credit than before. Indeed, letter grades can be safely abolished in favor of "credit" (for knowing a respectable amount of the material) and "no credit," or credit can be awarded in proportion to the amount of material learned.

DISTANCE LEARNING

A curricular design consisting of nuclear and planetary offerings simplifies, if it does not solve, some of the questions surrounding the value of "distance learning"—learning where the student is at a distance from the teacher. Here the computer and television are the media of instruction. Can these media, the question is, ever equal the interactivity of the classroom? Can electronic means ever duplicate the effectiveness of a real, live teacher?

The debate is on, and will last a long time. There can be no doubt that technology, which has already transformed day-to-day classroom administration, will be increasingly applied to every other aspect of teaching and learning. I strongly suspect, however, that no matter how "interactive" television and the computer may become, they will never be a match for the presence of an actual teacher in a small class. There are psychological and philosophical reasons for thinking that bodily presence is essential to the deepest human transactions. True discussion and debate, commitment to an argument, seem to depend on the actual presence of your interlocutor. If student involvement is the main key to learning, as researchers now insist, such involvement would naturally be best in close, personal interaction with teachers and other students. It is true that in particular situations a student may be less inhibited by the protection of "distance" from the instructor. In any case, no one to my knowledge is arguing that the electronic media are a *better* means of teaching than are small seminars.

This does not mean that technology does not have an important place. It does, and it is having a larger role in instruction than ever before. It will be used increasingly to serve remote and underprivileged audiences. It will no doubt also become progressively commercialized and debased. But it is also likely to become much more important to education of high quality, which seems destined to be a combination of classroom and media experiences. For the electronic media already share important traits with the traditional courses that have their place in the planetary area of the curriculum. Both, in a basic sense, are "distance learning." The lecture course, with the exception of the students' rare visits to office hours, is manifestly taught at a distance from the professor and has very few qualities that could not be duplicated by an excellent series on the Internet or television. Often even the medium-sized "discussion" course—every minute that the discussion veers to the other side of the room, every minute that the student is not personally involved in it, every minute that the student is bored or sleepy or misses a class—approaches the condition of distance learning.

But in its proper place—like the reading of a good book, which is similarly learning at a distance from the author—there is nothing wrong with distance learning. The principal strength of electronic media is precisely the vivid dissemination of that world of information situated around the nucleus of the curriculum. There is no reason why colleges—given that nucleus— should not then utilize such media as widely and economically as possible. It is true that, at this writing, colleges are not yet reporting significant savings in the use of electronic media, but that is because use so far is timid, and faculties are far from expert at it. Substantial future economies are inevitable. Computers are already widely used in putting out syllabi, class notices, and reading material, and in handling student questions; and younger professors are generally very much at ease at this level. Some universities are now webcasting excellent lecture courses for student convenience or as a public service. The growth of an "open-source" culture—such as exemplified by MIT's Open-CourseWare, Rice University's Connexions, and the Online Consortium of Independent Colleges and Universities directed by Regis University—suggests that a whole universe of excellent educational materials will soon be out there for the taking.

ECONOMY

The new curriculum involves important additional economies deriving from the general use of the small seminar. Because of the closeness with which students can be supervised, the seminar enables the decoupling of academic credit from seat time, connecting it to much more realistic measures. Anyone who has conducted a small seminar with properly firm standards knows that in it students are led to perform more *work*—whether it be in class discussion, reading, researching, field investigation, writing, or conferring with the professor—and to produce more verifiable educational results than in a conventional lecture or recitation course.

The conventional college semester course usually carries three units of credit, and students normally take five such courses per semester. When the seminar carries, as it should, academic credit commensurate with the actual work performed, it should generate a third to two-thirds more academic credit per student than a conventional course. In a nuclear seminar program, depending on how many seminars the student undertakes, the student in four years can earn the traditional amount of academic credit for the degree, with no diminution of academic quality, while enrolling in as many as five to ten fewer conventional courses. The economy in terms of faculty time is obvious. But there is also great economy of student time and energy. Every course a student removes from a highly proliferated course list saves the time taken up getting to and from the class, and the time and stress of extra tests and examinations; it also saves the administration a lot of bookkeeping. In the last generation, some of the more self-confident faculties, such as those at Harvard and Stanford, have tacitly adopted this logic by moving to four-unit courses, thus requiring no more than four courses per semester.

A curriculum requiring fewer courses for the degree is a distinct benefit to nontraditional students, steadily increasing in numbers, who do not have the traditional four full years at their disposal, and who may need the flexibility of hours that fit better into lives with family and job responsibilities.

What I have described above makes use of one resource that seems to have been consistently ignored, even though in times of financial stringency its promise of economies would seem to be inescapable. The truth is that while most faculties and administrations have a lamentable lack of funds, they have an unlimited supply of what is almost as good: *academic credit*. Faculties have been rightly jealous of the integrity of academic credit; nothing could be more contemptible than a cheap, unearned degree. But the same faculties that pride themselves on academic rigor ("excellence" is the current buzzword) have rarely paused to consider how lacking in rigor is the definition of academic credit that they almost universally employ.

One academic "unit," which like the dollar is currency from Maine to California and from college to college, means at present that in the fifteen-week semester system the student has engaged to park him- or herself in a classroom for one hour a week, done the assignments, and emerged from the course with a passing grade. Most courses that yield the conventional three units of credit thus require three hours of seat time per week. There is a widespread rule of thumb among professors that a student should also spend about two hours of study per week for each hour of class time. As for passing the course, it usually requires no more than a grade of C minus or D, that is, knowing about 65 or 70 percent of the material.

At its best, this conception produces only a modest return on the massive investment of time, talent, and energy that goes into supporting the typical curriculum. Factor into the transaction that only the most conscientious or terrified students actually spend this sort of time in class or do all the assignments. Indeed, in a 2004 large survey of undergraduates at so estimable a school as the University of California at Berkeley, students themselves claim to turn up in class only about 80 percent of the time, 30 percent report that they "often" or "very often" arrive in class without completing the readings or assignments, and another

37 percent admit to being "occasionally" delinquent. They also admit to completing only about 60 percent of the assigned course reading each year, and to spending barely seventeen hours each week (instead of the mythical thirty!) on out-of-class study activities such as assigned reading or writing, online or library research, lab work, and preparing for tests. "Furthermore," as the Duke Center for Academic Integrity reports, "Students everywhere use 'trots' or other shortcuts instead of reading the assignments, borrow lecture notes instead of processing the class material through their own minds, cram at the last minute for exams, and bargain with instructors for passing grades. There is widespread plagiarism of papers and cheating on exams."

Add to this the well-documented inflation of grades by faculties who at the same time paradoxically insist on "excellence," and the fact that barely half of full-time students at four-year colleges graduate after six years.

Even where the course material is "learned," the long-term results are often doubtful. According to a recent report done for the Carnegie Foundation for the Advancement of Teaching:

Research clearly shows that students have a lot of trouble understanding difficult concepts, often do not know how to use what they learn, and perhaps because they are not using that learning, tend to forget what they once knew. . . . In fact many college graduates cannot even remember what college courses they took. And sometimes students appear to remember the concepts they learned, but when asked to explain them, they reveal fundamental and persistent misconceptions. . . . Students often learn interpretations that conflict with their naive theories, but they learn them in the narrow context of the classroom and on a superficial level. When they are asked to explain or are confronted with a comparable issue outside the narrow context, their original misconceptions emerge intact.

The product of the present curriculum—despite a residue of good learning by good students in good courses—could hardly be called either excellent or economical.

The key to the efficient deployment of academic credit is the integrity of the teaching. Where learning is coupled with sympathetic and knowledgeable advising and closely supervised in small groups, the faculty is free to give credit where credit is due without the risk of cheapening the degree. Of course, there will always be professors who will regard *any* deviation from the conventional course as an escape from teaching. These will not be at home in the new environment.

THE ROLE OF THE FACULTY

With a curriculum combining nuclear seminars and planetary courses, the role of the faculty would be somewhat more complex than at present, but more interesting. Instead of simply offering some mixture of departmental and specialized courses on the undergraduate and graduate levels, professors would teach undergraduate interdisciplinary seminars and provide one or more other courses per term for the planetary curriculum or the graduate program. I use the term "provide," because if the curriculum takes full advantage of technology, the professor may not conventionally "teach" any given planetary course so much as be responsible for it. The professor may indeed choose to deliver lectures in person and also to webcast them for student use. Or he or she may choose a course from a media collection, make it available in that medium, arrange for whatever feedback to students is appropriate, and devise provisions for credit. In any case, it is likely that departmental planetary offerings, enrolling large numbers and providing introductory surveys or mainline subject matter for the general campus population rather than for majors, would curb the course proliferation and idiosyncrasy that at present characterizes the many departmental offerings driven by the narrow research interests of the faculty. Rather, current faculty scholarly interests—as long as they entail important questions, a lively openness to discussion and to fresh investigation—would produce ideal topics for the seminars. There would consequently be far more small undergraduate classes to teach than at present, many fewer middle-sized ones, and the large courses could be as large as practicable.

In this strategy college teachers would have greatly enlarged responsibilities for advising and for consulting with colleagues about the academic progress of the students they know in common. This will entail not only greater involvement in the actual intellectual lives of students but far greater collegiality within the faculty itself. Advisers must share information on the problems and accomplishments of individual students and become experts on what is available for those students from their colleagues in many fields. They will have more sensitive and arduous tasks of student evaluation, and they will be newly committed to the arts of course design and program evaluation, which will have to be radically strengthened if the commitment to intellectual training is to be taken seriously.

All these responsibilities will call for new resources of time and energy, and in many cases a new kind of professor. But they will fit snugly into a job free from the imperatives of specialist research for publication, and one where the professors' scholarship, in primary support of their status as teachers, will be the impulse and the occasion for the classes they teach and the intellectual guidance they provide.

THE ROLE OF THE STUDENT

In this configuration of studies, students would have more guidance, more freedom, and more responsibility. They would be guaranteed a hefty minimum of continuous supervised reading, research, speaking, and writing, and they would be kept close to their work by the intimacy of the seminar situation. But they would no longer be bound to the essentially unrealistic formula of the conventional curriculum—that a unit of credit requires an hour of formal instruction. Students would be judged and receive credit for the amount and quality of the work they did, rather than by the amount of time they sat in the classroom. Thus, while they might in fact spend considerable time (say, three to five hours) per week in seminar, the rest of their work could be performed elsewhere, and according to their own schedules. If some of their concurrent planetary courses were made available electronically, students would have extraordinary flexibility in the management of their time.

Exposure to a succession of seminar teachers would give the student continuously close academic advising and, finally, the opportunity to choose from the faculty the person who could most capably guide the student to and through the senior project. In this sense, each student would have an individual major. The student would not have to take a series of required "departmental major" courses so much as come to agreement with the adviser on the best possible course of study. Faculty critics of "general" or individual or field majors usually complain that the students end up knowing a little about a lot of things but not much about anything. And this can be very true in the conventional academic curriculum. But the criticism is baseless where responsible faculty advising ultimately leads the student's interest to a real focus, and where the student is in any case practiced beyond the ordinary in intellectual skills. Indeed, it is arguable that a well-thought-out program of individual studies leading to a focused project would produce more genuine intellectual depth than the typical major made up of an often-random accumulation of courses whose only coherence arises from their having been offered by the same academic department.

Nothing would prevent the student's ultimate choice of a specialization similar to the conventional departmental major, especially if the major had been reformed to provide coherence, community, and depth. As I have suggested, this would most likely be in the case of a student who has made an early decision to pursue a career within academia. But most students would enjoy the freedom to move up from seminar to seminar, that is, from problem to problem, sometimes changing directions, crossing borders, testing different areas and fields of interest, until they came upon the topic that would focus their most mature college work.

ASSESSMENT

No curriculum will have lasting value unless we know whether it works. What do our students actually learn? Which are our best teachers? Our best programs? And in the same terms, which are our best colleges? "Assessment" has been proliferating steadily in American colleges for the past thirty years, but we are still far from having a reliable notion of how successful college education actually is. We have had for a while a deep intimation that our students do not learn as well as they could, that our colleges are not really doing the job. It is this intimation—especially on the part of legislators, prospective employers, and paying parents—that has exerted an ever-increasing pressure on colleges, especially the public ones, to provide evidence that they are worth the massive amounts of tuition and of public money they cost.

Colleges have perforce needed to respond to this pressure and have engaged in a variety of assessment activities aided by substantial work by professional researchers. The literature on assessment is already vast, but there is nothing nearly resembling general use of reliable and sophisticated assessment of college education. "Assessment" of the work of students by their own teachers in the form of letter grading is almost universal, as is peer rating of research achievement of faculty for appointment or promotion. Rating of teachers by their own students—however unreliable except as a measure of satisfaction—is very common. But only a few colleges do refined assessment of student learning, and rating of faculty by their colleagues or other competent judges for teaching achievement is more honored in the breach than in the observance.

Over a thousand colleges have used the annual National Survey of Student Engagement administered at the University of Indiana and based on student questionnaires emphasizing activities that are expected to generate engagement. The Council for Aid to Education of the Rand Corporation has sponsored a Collegiate Learning Assessment Project. It "focuses on student learning" and is "based on the institution" and "on the value-added provided by colleges and universities." It has been widely praised, adopted by some hundreds of colleges, and generously supported by the Teagle Foundation. Its methodology, however, is still problematic.

In any case, assessment of whole programs is infrequent, and we have virtually no reliable assessment of the teaching power of individual colleges. Annual rankings of colleges by such publications as *U.S. News and World Report* are based largely on testimony by administrators who seldom have firsthand knowledge, and on statistics that have little relevance to learning. Actually, the response of the elite, research-oriented universities to the call for assessment has been minimal, usually limited to providing statistics on such items as library expenditures, entrance scores, and graduation rates, which are irrelevant to the question, and on faculty/student ratios and class sizes, which might be more relevant if the numbers were reliable. In terms of the power to teach undergraduates, the faculty/student ratio is meaningless if the faculty isn't teaching; and average class sizes can be statistically shrunk by a variety of means, such as by counting section meetings and tutorials as "classes," by fielding a large number of small, low-credit "seminars," or by including graduate seminars in the calculations.

In this sort of ambience, even where administrators have safely provided statistics, their faculties may not have responded at all. Either they have not even heard of public demands for accountability, or they reject them as impudence. Among some of the faculties of elite institutions, where "excellence" reigns automatically and arrogance mixes comfortably with complacency, to question the value of what professors do is simply ignorant, or "anti-intellectual," or a potential threat to academic freedom. Meanwhile, they typically cannot supply reliable evidence for the educational effectiveness of a single one of their courses.

Lesser institutions have generally done better with assessment, and many public institutions have had to assess themselves in one way or another in response to legislation. Many of them chafe under the burden of standardized assessment "instruments" which are not designed for their particular programs and in which they have no confidence. Legislators often have rather primitive views of what education is supposed to be, and mandate measurements of the kinds of programs they themselves went through as students. Such measurements are largely quantitative; for educators who regard education as something beyond remembering subject matter, they are nearly useless.

A 1998 survey responded to by about half (1,393) of the postsecondary institutions in the country showed that

> institutions most often collect data on objective, easily obtained indicators like student progress (96 percent), academic plans (88 percent), or satisfaction (74 percent) rather than measures of student cognitive or affective development. . . .
>
> Relatively few institutions reported conducting studies of the relationship between various institutional experiences and student performance, and almost 40 percent reported doing no such studies. The most common studies were management-oriented, examining the relationship of admissions policies (42 percent) and financial aid policies (30 percent) with student performance. Relatively few institutions examined relationships of educational experiences (such as course patterns, advising, extracurricular activities, teaching methods, and academic resources) and student performance. And, by far, the least amount of attention was given to the relationship of student and faculty interaction with student performance— one of the variables known to have the greatest impact.

This study suggests that whereas excellence in undergraduate education is often stressed in an institution's mission (82 percent), a focus on student outcomes (52 percent) is less often mentioned, and student assessment as an institutional priority (19 percent) is usually not included.

Despite this partial, half-hearted response to the call for

accountability, assessment nevertheless remains one of the most important tasks confronting college education today; it is also one of the most difficult. It poses profound questions of scholarship. Learning and its goals are extremely complex, hard to define at best, and subject to a wide range of opinion. The effects of college courses are hard to distinguish from the effects of extracurricular experiences, including natural maturation. Students come with a great range of backgrounds and talents, and they may respond unreliably to efforts at assessment. But assessment is imperative. There is something almost grotesque in the widespread failure of the academic establishment to study its own central activity. Apart from supporting the public claims of the system as a whole, assessment is crucial internally. It is essential to maintaining a sound curriculum, to providing students with nourishing feedback, and to recognizing professors who are good teachers.

Assessment of Students

Among all the possible kinds of assessment, assessment of student learning is by far the most important. Without it, the others will yield questionable, if not irrelevant, results. If you do not know, as directly as possible, how well your students are learning, you cannot really tell who is a good teacher, what is a good course or program, and ultimately, how good your college is. Conversely, reliable information on the learning of individual students can be the basis for confident evaluation of faculty, for sound course and curriculum planning, and for reliable rating of colleges.

This is no more than common sense, but unless you have, as some educators do, a simplistically quantitative notion of what learning is all about, it is damnably difficult to achieve. The learning we are concerned with here is mostly qualitative. Beyond the factual material, what do we want students to learn? And how do we find out if they do?

No college has asked and answered these questions better than Alverno, a small Catholic liberal arts college for women in Milwaukee. The college has earned worldwide attention for putting assessment at its center. Beginning in the 1970s with a continuous study of what outcome it wanted from each of its programs, Alverno has carried assessment so deeply into its practice that it is not only an institutional device but "an essential contributing part of each student's learning process." The college has come to the profound view that "assessment is integral to learning." Nothing of consequence occurs in its curriculum that is not validated by assessment of some kind. To arrive at this position the faculty has given its best answers to the key educational questions and followed up their consequences with hard work and steady integrity. Its study of assessment has been continuous and evolving, and it has produced generous publications on the subject.

Alverno does not use tests, exams, or other conventional graded assignments as such. For the bachelor's degree, each student must have demonstrated eight abilities: communication, analysis, problem solving, valuing in decision-making, social interaction, global perspectives, effective citizenship, and aesthetic responsiveness. Each of these abilities is explicitly and publicly defined, as are the six levels of each. The student is expected to demonstrate these abilities—in a variety of different settings—as she passes through her studies. All the assessments are designed to validate able performance—the college emphasizes *doing* what you know about—on the basis of clear and public criteria. They thus involve the design and evaluation of a great variety of written, oral, and group-based student activities, including portfolios, projects, papers, surveys, demonstrations, presentations, interviews. The assessments are administered mostly by faculty but may also include the student's peers, advanced students, alumnae, and members of the professional community.

Although the college maintains "ability departments" designed to support campuswide attention to each of the eight abilities, it is still—to my mind unnecessarily—organized around departmental majors. But at Alverno each academic discipline is closely analyzed for its specific contribution to the abilities, and the major effectively consists of the student's attaining the highest ability levels in that disciplinary context.

Alverno engages the student's collaboration from the beginning of the program: "We, in effect, let students in on the learning and assessment process so that they can gradually take their development into their own hands" (20).

For us, most indicative of a student's achievement of educational goals are signs that she is learning to learn, especially that she has become an increasingly self directed learner. Patterns we have found in the advanced development of students' self assessment ability emerge with increasing frequency. A student suggests her progression in this regard when she consistently applies self awareness and formative evaluations of her work. She emphasizes reliance on self evaluation and gives evidence of internalizing standards of self assessment. . . .

All of this is specifically fostered by the very nature of assessment as we define and practice it, since self assessment is an integral part of each assessment instrument and/or process in which the student participates, and is assessed as an ability she is developing. As a student progresses, she is also required to take a greater and greater share of initiative in deciding which learning experiences she needs. . . . In her advanced work a student participates increasingly in the design of her learning experiences and assessment. (75–76)

One of the main goals of assessment, then, is to establish the student's capacity for self-assessment, and studies show that this goal can be achieved to a satisfying extent.

Alverno's success in this area clearly involves a profound reconception of the job of an undergraduate teaching faculty. In addition to expertise in their disciplinary field of study, Alverno faculty must become experts in assessment as well as in learning theory and practice. The remarkable persistence and integrity with which this modestly paid faculty has pursued over many decades the ideal of self-assessment for itself suggest the benign influence of its Franciscan connections; it has practiced what it preached. While its energy can hardly be imagined as a norm for American faculties, it shows that an effectively new curriculum anywhere will require a newly educated and newly dedicated teaching staff.

The Alverno example shows too—as does recent study of other successful efforts—that whether or not student assessment on a given campus begins with a need for accountability, it should be designed foremost to improve instruction; in a deep sense, it is essential to learning. It should be a central commitment of the faculty and should engage the collaboration of students as early as possible. It should be based on shared, valued purposes and clearly stated program objectives, and it should be designed as an ongoing activity. To this end, each campus should have at its center an office, manned by competent scholars, devoted to continuous study of the college itself.

Assessment of Faculty

The greatest obstacle to rewarding the teaching achievement of faculty, and thus to placing teaching in its proper place above research in the priorities of colleges, has been how hard it is to document teaching ability. The publication record is *there*, in black and white. Furthermore, it is portable, internationally if necessary, and is thus an essential aid to mobility between jobs. The teaching record, by contrast, is strictly local, inhering mainly in the impressions and memories of students and colleagues. At best, it makes the professors celebrities (or prisoners) in their present institution. So, whatever their subscription to the importance of teaching, colleges have found it convenient to judge by what is by far the easier to assess. Teaching *is* brought into the equation, of course, but only pro forma. The usual question, effectively, is whether or not there is any serious trouble. For this, highly unreliable student questionnaires, the unstudied opinions of colleagues, and perhaps a review of course materials are deemed sufficient. The 1998 survey mentioned above reports that "for faculty decisions related to promotion, tenure, and rewards, student assessment data are apparently not used."

One of the greatest benefits of a good assessment program is that it makes newly clear—in fact, it is built upon—what the college or the department or the course is teaching *for*. In a college culture in which everyone—the students included—was aware of specific, public, agreed-upon educational goals, the aims of instruction would be clearer, and the results of teaching more concrete and therefore more open to reliable assessment. Even such a traditional and widespread device as student evaluation of courses would gain new validity. If every student had a good idea of what the course's aims were, the end-of-term questionnaire would become less a popularity poll and more an informed response.

A better system of assessing teaching ability would have to be based on a reconception of what it means to be a member of a teaching faculty. As with research, assessment of teaching is most reliably done in a peer environment, that is, in an environment of fellow teachers. At present, teaching is mostly a solo activity; professors devise and teach their own courses and are seldom visited by colleagues. Even in departmental courses— where various professors teach sections of the same required course—they seldom collaborate closely on the progress of the course, much less on its results. So colleagues generally have little on which to base reliable judgment of each other's teaching.

In a college where teaching was seen as the main job of work, the situation could be much different. The design, progress, and results of each course would be a prime subject of interest to all. Ideas would be freely interchanged. Group planning would be the rule, and intervisitation would be as permissible and natural as reading each other's writings. In this atmosphere, even the traditional methods of evaluating teachers would have a new authenticity. Personal statements would be more meaningful, as would colleagues' recommendations and portfolios containing syllabi, examinations, and other teaching materials. Above all, in the presence of well-understood, commonly held pedagogical goals, faculties and their committees could begin to relate the assessment of student work to the skills of individual teachers.

Toward a New Curriculum
COLLEGES WITH INNOVATIVE FEATURES

Despite the formidable obstacles, the new curriculum *is* slowly making its way into American colleges. The logic of new thinking has become too powerful to be ignored wherever student learning is a primary concern. Confidently, if perhaps optimistically, the Association of American Colleges and Universities has announced the emergence of the "new academy." Robert B. Barr and John Tagg have described lucidly and in detail "a new paradigm for undergraduate education," and many colleges have experimented with or adopted one or another feature of it. Examining the whole range of innovative curricula, one expectably finds a miscellany, from a few courses to whole programs, varying widely as to how many innovative traits they have, and whether they have enough coherence and leverage to produce a powerful education for undergraduates. Prospective college students and their parents would be well advised to consider seriously those colleges, such as the ones mentioned in this chapter, which demonstrate genuine attention to putting students first. Our four-year private liberal arts colleges, as a group, are educationally by far the strongest sector.

Alexander Astin reports that "residential liberal arts colleges in general, and highly selective liberal arts colleges in particular, produce a pattern of consistently positive student outcomes not found in any other type of American higher education institution. . . . [They] have managed not only to effect a reasonable balance between undergraduate teaching and scholarly research, but also to incorporate a wide range of exemplary educational practices. " Often the central ethos of a college has involved so deep a commitment to student learning to start with that the continuing tradition of the college—or in some cases a crisis in its health—has produced reforms. Sensitive administrators with a committed faculty over the years have discovered some of the best pedagogical ideas and gradually assimilated them. In any case, these colleges have a greater ability to change. With their relative political independence, and their comparative freedom from the research mania, they can be depended upon to continue their leadership in teaching and learning. But however visible some of them may be, they are teaching a very small proportion—less than 5 percent—of our college students.

Establishing innovative arrangements in a large, research-oriented institution, on the other hand, is as rare as it is difficult. For the most part, such institutions have produced only minor tinkering with the undergraduate curriculum. At many major research universities, every decade or two someone has a crisis of conscience about the undergraduate curriculum. Committees are appointed, hearings are held, and a report is published and discussed by the faculty and then placed safely on file, rarely to be heard of again. Existing innovations tend to be modest, located mostly on the edges of the curriculum, often looking like concessions or compromises barely wrested from the departmental faculty. They are often staffed by faculty "borrowed" part-time from departments, or by temporary part-time faculty, supplemented by graduate students and even undergraduates. Unless they have been given the rare status of schools or departments, their staffs and courses operate at an obvious disadvantage in terms of appointment, promotion, planning, and funding.

The University of Pennsylvania faculty recently ran a four-year pilot program testing a new general education curriculum, so far with inconclusive results. Yale has at least produced a successful new program of freshman seminars. More promising yet, the faculty of Harvard College has recently made a fundamental change in the undergraduate curriculum that may well be even more important than those enacted by the fabled Harvard Report of 1945. Harvard has of course a virtually automatic influence on other large research universities, including the would-be Harvards that aspire to "national ranking." Faculties all over the nation will shortly be considering Harvard's decision. What is even more important, however, is that the change—unlike those of 1945—responds directly to the conclusions about student learning that I have just called "new thinking." It implicitly challenges basic features of the conventional undergraduate curriculum. Since the faculties of the undergraduate colleges of most big universities have thus far been woodenly impervious to innovation, the prospect of Harvard's influence is unusually important.

The old Harvard Core Program—which required all students to take seven courses selected from subject areas outside their concentration—is abolished. In its place is a new General Education Curriculum. What is fundamental about this change is that the new curriculum does not call simply for discipline-based courses but for courses that will educate for four broad goals: prepare students for civic engagement; teach students to understand themselves as products of—and participants in—traditions of art, ideas, and values; prepare students to respond critically and constructively to change; and develop students' understanding of the ethical dimensions of what they say and do.

In pursuit of these goals the faculty specifies eight areas of study from each of which students must take one course. The criteria for these courses are heavily weighted toward skills, toward the confrontation of problems, and toward application to student experience.

There is almost nothing not to like in Harvard's plan. It is aimed squarely at student involvement, and at the study of issues and problems, not the mere ingestion of academic subject matter. It answers brilliantly to the faculty's desire to provide "a general education curriculum that is responsive to the conditions of the twenty-first century":

We face the challenge of preparing our students to lead flourishing and productive lives in a world that is dramatically different from the world in which most of us grew up. The world today is interconnected to a degree almost inconceivable thirty or forty years ago. It is, and in ways that are often obscured in the press and the culture of public life, a deeply divided, unstable, and uncertain world. Harvard's students will need to make their way in an environment complex for new and incompletely understood reasons; they will also lead lives that will affect the lives of others.

But while I applaud the faculty, and sympathize with the committees that will now have to recruit faculty and come up with courses that genuinely answer to the new criteria, a big question remains: *Why are these changes, these splendid goals, limited to so small a part of the students' schedules, a mere quarter of their course work?* Why shouldn't these General Education requirements—designed to produce responsible citizens who are armed with the skills to cope with a complex world—why shouldn't they be the substantial heart and center of the student's experience, instead of a scattering of courses at its periphery? Why has the Harvard faculty seemingly stopped so short of the full implementation of its own logic?

The answer of course is that the Harvard faculty is an aggregation primarily assembled for and devoted to research, not undergraduate learning, and this is as far as its enlightened study committees could push it.

Almost a hundred other colleges have modified their "core" curricula—the courses required of all students—by adding interdisciplinary courses to or substituting them for the standard distribution among arts, humanities, social science, natural science, and mathematics courses. This suggests that trying to provide students with "breadth" by requiring a number of discrete courses in each of the major areas of learning has fallen into a certain constructive disrepute. A generally wide choice of courses within each area means that what students actually learn is unpredictable, that the chosen courses have little relationship to each other, and that students have little intellectual experience in common. The requirement, furthermore, is often the occasion for enrollment competition among the divisions of the college. Among the colleges that have adopted the most broadly based interdisciplinary core curricula are Adelphi, Appalachian State and Watunga College, Chestnut Hill, Colgate, Concordia, Dartmouth, Hollins, McMurry, Ohio University, Olivet, Portland State, St. Andrews, Sonoma State, Texas A&M at Corpus Christi, Ursinus, Wheaton, and Valparaiso.

Even in the large research universities, the idea of interdisciplinary studies has become almost popular, partly owing to its power within the area of research itself. As President John Sexton of NYU has recently put it, "One of the best tools for inquiry and insight is examining intellectual formulations and artistic acts, not just with colleagues in the same discipline, wherever they are located, but from the perspective of colleagues both within and outside one's discipline—and present at one's own university."

Some increasingly dominant subjects—such as area studies, period studies, women's studies, ethnic studies, media studies, urban studies, environmental studies, public health, and the like—are inherently interdisciplinary. Other subjects, such as bioethics and bioengineering, have been yoked into existence by special urgencies of modern life. Whatever the circumstances, the term "interdisciplinary" seems almost everywhere to connote an expectation of added refreshment along with added intellectual power. Interdisciplinary studies are proving to be most congenially applicable to civic engagement programs, especially for first-year students. Most notable is the program at New Century College of George Mason University. The First-Year Experience program consists of four consecutive interdisciplinary team-taught courses conducted in small seminars, using collaborative assignments, and fulfilling almost all the college's "core" requirements.

There is a well-established Association of Integrative Studies, centered at Miami University, in Oxford, Ohio, with a membership of five hundred colleges that offer interdisciplinary studies; it has published a four-hundred-page directory of undergraduate programs. Interdisciplinary studies has itself become a topic of research and of graduate education. Most significantly, Arizona State University has recently converted its Department of Anthropology into a new interdisciplinary, problem-oriented School of Human Evolution and Social Change.

The New College of Interdisciplinary Arts and Sciences at Arizona State University West offers a mixture of traditional and innovative programs. Among the most promising of the latter are Integrative Studies and Interdisciplinary Social Sciences. The core requirements for the B.A. in Integrative Studies include courses from groups entitled Ethical Reflection, Diverse Identities, Scientific and Mathematical Perspectives, and Secular and Sacred Worldviews, and a capstone project involving field experience, research, or writing. The student's "area of concentration" may be a disciplinary minor or be constructed individually. In Interdisciplinary Social Sciences, in addition to interdisciplinary courses in theory and methodology and an optional but recommended senior thesis, the major calls for substantial study in three course clusters: Identity/Difference, Power/Knowledge, and Local/Global. The department envisions these clusters as addressing key social issues.

A similar popularity has attached itself to the idea of undergraduate seminars, including freshman seminars. Google recently listed many hundreds of thousands of references to "undergraduate seminar," "senior seminar," and "freshman seminar." It is clear that the manifold needs of entering students—not only curricular needs but also needs relating to the adjustment to college life, to the particular campus, and to unfamiliar student populations—have particularly called forth seminar arrangements. Undergraduate seminars, then, vary widely in their content, timing, duration, amount of academic credit given, and teaching staff. The Creative Inquiry program at Clemson University keeps students together for several semesters, and combines the seminar idea with the growing recognition of the power of undergraduate research projects.

The idea of student engagement and student community as supports for learning has generated promising movements—particularly strong among community colleges—toward community-based learning, service learning, and "learning communities." Learning communities vary widely in character and scope. The principal organizers and reporters of this movement use the term to

refer to a variety of curricular approaches that intentionally link or cluster two or more courses, often around an interdisciplinary theme or problem, and enroll a common cohort of students. They represent an intentional restructuring of students' time, credit, and learning experiences to build community, enhance learning, and foster connections among students, faculty, and disciplines. At their best, learning communities practice pedagogies of active engagement and reflection. On residential campuses, many learning communities are also living-learning communities, restructuring the residential environment to build community and integrate academic work with out-of-class experience.

In learning communities, students and faculty members might examine, for example, technology and human values, war and peace, the Renaissance, or American pluralism. In all, however, students and teachers experience courses and disciplines as a complementary whole, not as arbitrary or isolated offerings.

A pioneering program, called Federated Learning Communities, was early established at an otherwise traditional institution, SUNY Stony Brook, by Patrick Hill, who later went on to play a key role at Evergreen State. At present, the yearlong program focuses on a major issue, such as world hunger, creativity, gender and sexual diversity, or globalism. For two semesters students take three regular university courses relevant to the issue and a substantial program seminar that integrates the material.

Each seminar is led by a regular faculty member, called a "master learner," who actually takes the three courses—exams, papers, and all—and acts as a model for the students. Students may earn a minor in the program.

Yet another variation of the learning community is the University of Oregon's Freshman Interest Groups. There are some fifty of these groups, which operate in the fall term. Each brings together twenty-five first-year students who take the same two regular university core courses and also meet in a one-credit course typically taught by a faculty member assisted by student mentors. The learning communities at Arizona State University West Campus similarly provide first-time freshmen with two academic courses (for instance, political science/psychology, ethnic studies/composition, English/history) and a one-credit integrative seminar taught by the course instructors. Each learning community is supported by a librarian, a technology specialist, a teaching assistant, and a peer mentor. The College of the Holy Cross, which also has a well-developed Center for Interdisciplinary and Special Studies, offers yearlong interdisciplinary seminars to small groups of first-year students, who also live together.

Most deeply committed to the idea of community is the Bailey Scholars Program at Michigan State, which offers a specialization in Connected Learning. The curriculum is anchored in three highly collaborative, student-controlled core seminars. While allowing great freedom of choice of studies, the program requires students to have a learning plan and portfolio, to maintain strong contact with their various communities both on and off campus, and to remain continuously aware of their learning goals.

The University of Washington's Interdisciplinary Writing Program links seminars in expository writing, taught by writing instructors, with lecture courses in various humanities and social science departments. The writing assignments are based on the materials in the linked course and can include drafts of course papers. Even closer integration of instruction in writing with academic subject matter is achieved in the highly successful Writing Workshop Program at Tufts University. Writing Workshop (WW) courses, offered in almost every academic department, are not simply writing courses but rather versions of already established courses, taught by departmental faculty specially trained in WW techniques. Fifteen to twenty courses, with a maximum of twenty students each, are offered each semester. Students are expected to work closely with each other and the instructor as they define topics and revise drafts. Additionally, many WW courses offer students practice in public speaking.

Some colleges now offer alternative, interdisciplinary majors, many of them featuring seminar work. MIT offers a minor and a joint major (along with a well-developed graduate program) in Science, Technology, and Society. The Western College Program at Miami University offers degrees in Interdisciplinary Studies and in Environmental Studies. Students live together and under close faculty supervision design their own research topics and senior projects. The University of Chicago's New Collegiate Division offers four interdisciplinary concentrations: Environmental Studies; Issues and Texts, which centers on intensive study of a few classic texts; Law, Letters, and Society; and a completely individualized Tutorial Studies. At the University of Redlands, two hundred students live together in the Johnston Center for Integrative Studies. They write contracts for courses, design their own majors, and receive narrative evaluation in place of grades. The Center for Interdisciplinary Studies at Davidson College provides collegewide interdisciplinary seminars and coordinates student-designed majors in such fields as neuroscience, film studies, poverty and development, international relations, medical humanities, environmental policy, genomics, comparative religion, East Asian studies, and health care ethics.

Some colleges have encapsulated their innovative arrangements within special "honors programs" or "honors colleges," usually open only to "qualified" students, who receive all manner of special treatment. These programs are widely used to attract donors, enhance the college's attractiveness to exceptionally well prepared applicants, or provide a comfortable refuge in the midst of the ordinary curriculum for students who are regarded as particularly self-motivated and intellectually inclined.

In addition to interdepartmental majors, such as Environmental Thought and Practice, the University of Virginia offers an interdisciplinary major program for students with "superior ability." They design their own programs and produce a two-semester senior thesis "that should certainly go beyond, or perhaps be outside, any course given."

A notable honors program is that of King's College, where qualified students attend special classes limited to fifteen students. They take an eight-course "humanities suite" in the first two years, four honors seminars thereafter, and in their senior year do research leading up to an honors thesis. Honors students may carry out independent study projects and, in place of the usual departmental major, may elect to design individual majors.

At the Lee Honors College of Western Michigan University, students take, in addition to conventional academic majors, two two-course clusters in the freshman and sophomore years. The courses, in small seminar format, are clustered around a general theme, such as Ethics, Science, and the Environment, or Politics of the 20th Century: The Dehumanization of the Other. The courses "focus on writing, primary sources, group discussion, and critical thinking, and . . . foster intellectual connections among these courses." In the junior and senior years students take at least two interdisciplinary seminars on critical issues (e.g., Risk-Taking and Change, Social Inequality in the U.S. and Latin America) "to continue to develop [their] problem-solving abilities and their competence in considering and using other areas of study to analyze a complex issue." Finally, they produce a senior research thesis "typical of professional work in a major field."

New College of the University of Alabama is limited to two hundred students. They plan and contract for their own concentrations, called depth study, and fulfill most of their core require-ments in a graded series of five integrative seminars based on problems drawn from the humanities, social science, and natu-ral science. They are also encouraged to do at least one semester of directed out-of-class learning or independent study.

While applauding the creation of honors programs such as these, one may be permitted to wonder why they are ever re-stricted, why any students are ever barred from trying out intel-lectually attractive special programs. We probably underestimate how many students are confirmed in their lack of interest by the very mediocrity of the curricula in which they are penned, and would indeed respond positively if offered a more powerful envi-ronment for learning.

One college that has addressed this question very success-fully is the College of Wooster in Ohio. Wooster has had since 1948 an independent study program that has so penetrated the whole college culture as to give it unique distinction. For the B.A. degree, all students take a first-year seminar in critical inquiry and complete a departmental or student-designated major. But each in addition also designs and produces an independent study thesis (written work, artifact, or performance), supported by a junior course in research skills and methods, and a two-course senior tutorial with a faculty adviser. Students start think-ing about their "IS" projects in lower division, and it engages a disproportional amount of their attention and energy there-after; they produce a prodigious range of projects.

The remarkable Howard Lowry, president of Wooster from 1944 to 1967, who modeled this program on one at Princeton, insisted that it be required of all students. "Independent study is not reserved for the intellectually elite alone," he wrote.

> The new program is democratic and aristocratic at once—
> aristocratic in that it challenges a student to come to his
> own best; democratic, in that it offers the opportunity
> and challenge to everyone. . . . Every man and woman is
> potentially an honors candidate, allowed the chance to
> find himself even after a possibly slow start. . . . the hon-

ors man frequently turns out . . . to be the shy average boy of freshman and sophomore year who never would have dared propose himself for anything beyond routine class work and whom the faculty, in its statistical wisdom, would have rejected anyhow as unpromising honors material. Somehow, once participating in his own project, learning not merely from lectures but from competent faculty guides and friends who deal with him about his problems and show him how to make his special kind of improvement, many a student has sounded his own true depth.

Wooster has buttressed the success of the program with a generous provision for advising. All faculty work with IS students, one on one, and receive course credit for a reasonable number of advisees. They also benefit from an enlightened faculty development policy; it provides generously for both conventional research leaves and study leaves, "to support professional growth by faculty members through defined plans of study, and thus to enhance their teaching and afford students the opportunity to study under the inspiration and guidance of faculty members who are actively engaged with scholarship in their fields."

The payoff for these and related attributes of the college has been a remarkable record of student scholarship, the retention of good faculty, and a mounting reputation. As Loren Pope remarks in *Colleges That Change Lives:* "Wooster has been producing achievers for a long time: it's a college that has never been particularly selective, often accepting 80% to 90% of its applicants, yet it ranks number 11 among all the 914 colleges in the country in the percentage of graduates who go on to get Ph.D.s. And it has done this for three quarters of a century."

The New Curriculum
SOME INNOVATIVE COLLEGES

Independent whole colleges having a new curriculum have appeared on a few large university campuses where the presence of a research faculty has not prevented granting to new collegiate structures enough autonomy to set up and prove themselves. Administered as an independent school, the University Professors Program (UNI) of Boston University begins freshman year with core-course seminars and a year-long weekly gathering to discuss research papers presented by the faculty. The student then takes course work leading to a substantial interdisciplinary senior thesis and oral defense. Similarly independent, New College, part of the University of South Florida, requires its highly selected students to contract personally for each semester's program. Contracts include projected work in courses, tutorials, and independent reading; three required month-long independent study projects; and in the junior year an area of concentration, which may be divisional, disciplinary, or individual, concluding with a senior thesis and oral exam. Courses change frequently; classes are small, averaging seventeen students, and are taught by professors only; professors provide narrative evaluations instead of letter grades.

Fairhaven College was purposely designed as the innovative unit of Western Washington University, and it fulfills this role with distinctive energy. It is interdisciplinary and issue oriented, emphasizes both community and self-direction, and serves students of widely diverse ages, ethnic origins, academic goals, and life experiences. All of its evaluations of faculty, including reviews for appointment, tenure, and promotion, are college-based.

At Fairhaven, the curriculum is engaged in both process and subject matter, and most courses pay attention to both. In addition to freshman introductory seminars entitled Interdisciplinary Study, Critical and Reflective Inquiry, and Social Relationships and Responsibility, students take a series of six required core seminars, distributed among three groups: Humanities and the Expressive Arts, Society and the Individual, and Science and Our Place on the Planet. Most of these courses lean toward the interdisciplinary and toward provocative themes, with titles such as Art and Social Issues, Palestine, and Human Interaction with Natural Systems.

About 70 percent of students create their own major (or Fairhaven Concentration), which "integrates the contributions of several disciplines to a problem, issue or theme." Fairhaven believes in giving students unusual freedom in designing their programs, but it also believes in close advising and firm student orientation at every step of the way. For help in demonstrating readiness to pursue concentrated studies and in developing their concentration proposal, students attend a transition conference, and a seminar in which they actually write the proposal. They discuss with each other and individually with advisers such questions as, What do you want to achieve in your degree? Who should be on your committee? and, How do the parts of your concentration work together conceptually? Ten to twenty-five percent of a student's concentration is done through independent study projects, but each project requires a careful written proposal, including a statement of qualifications, approved by a faculty sponsor. The concentration is capped with a senior project and an advanced seminar in which the student produces a summary and evaluation of his or her work in the major.

No letter grades are given at Fairhaven. Students write a self-evaluation of their performance at the end of each course, and faculty respond with a written evaluation of the student's progress, which becomes part of the student's permanent portfolio and a credential for employment or graduate school. Joint evaluations are also used in the writing portfolio, which begins with a writing plan drawn up as early as the foundations seminar and contains representative examples of a student's work that are reviewed by faculty for substance, structure, and style.

Fairhaven's capacity to innovate is further illustrated by the Law and Diversity Program, which prepares students from underrepresented ethnic, social, or economic groups to enter the legal profession. Emphasis is placed on the development of skills essential to legal thinking: critical reading, writing, research, oral communication, and analytical ability. Each entering class is formed into a separate "cohort," an ongoing, supportive learning community.

Students hold voting membership on all Fairhaven committees and in general are encouraged to speak up and make their ideas known. The result is a remarkable liveliness in seminar discussions, and a sense of community and involvement that permeates the whole college.

The curriculum at New York University's Gallatin School of Individualized Study is based on an elegantly constructed "expansive notion of the great books." Students in the undergraduate program spend from a quarter to a half of their studies in their own concentration, "organized around a theme, problem, activity, period of history, area of the world, or some central idea." They take, concurrently, a series of two thematically organized writing seminars leading to a long research paper, and four interdisciplinary seminars, beginning with a first-year seminar.

These small classes of about twenty students encourage discussion rather than lecturing and use interesting writing exercises rather than conventional examinations. Each of the seminars focuses on a theme—such as Creativity, Masters and Servants, Pilgrimage and Sacred Places, and Masculine/Feminine—incorporating great books and significant texts representing several disciplines.

Advanced seminars (almost 200 of them) focus on "significant books and various themes in the history of ideas." The program also provides for independent study, tutorials, internships, courses in other NYU programs, and—in the unparalleled New York area—private lessons. Through the seminars and other courses, students fulfill a liberal arts core requirement covering humanities, social science, and either mathematics or science. They also start preparing early for the "colloquium," a final two-hour oral examination (or conversation) with three members of the faculty, based on an integrated list of twenty to twenty-five books representing a variety of disciplines and historical periods, including those relevant to their concentration. Prior to the colloquium they write a brief rationale, describing the themes they intend to discuss.

Some independent colleges have managed to transform their entire curriculum, and others have been created to be innovative from scratch. Among the former, besides Alverno College (see above, chap. 4) perhaps the most famous and successful is St. John's, the third oldest college in the country, with campuses in Annapolis and Santa Fe. In 1937 it adopted a unique curriculum based on the ideas of Robert M. Hutchins, of the University of Chicago, and has been faithful to it ever since. St. John's has one of the most highly prescriptive curricula, which is nevertheless innovative in that it is interdisciplinary, problem oriented, and based on seminars and tutorials. All students take the same four years of team-taught seminars in which they confront problems based on "the great books of the Western tradition." They also take, in tutorials of fifteen students, four years of language (Greek and French), four years of math, three years of lab science, and one year of music. The only lecture they must attend comes on Friday evenings, when the entire college listens to and afterward questions a faculty member or visiting speaker.

There are a growing number of small colleges entirely devoted to study of the environment. At College of the Atlantic in Bar Harbor, Maine, all students major in human ecology, and pursue individual majors and research projects in the field and in interdisciplinary seminars.

Among the oldest and most successful of designedly innovative colleges is Bennington, founded on Deweyan principles as a women's college in Vermont in 1932; it began admitting men in 1969. After an impressive start—its early faculty included such creative giants as Martha Graham, José Limón, W. H. Auden, Erich Fromm, Buckminster Fuller, and Peter Drucker—it fell after mid-century into a gradual decline, acquiring a reputation for being not only the most expensive college in the country but a somewhat odd one to boot. Administrative crises, deficits, dwindling enrollment, and faculty self-entrenchment led in 1987 to the appointment of Elizabeth Coleman as president. Since then the college has recovered brilliantly. In 1994 the Bennington trustees published a symposium report, the result of strenuous research and discussion aimed at re-creating the college in accordance with its original principles:

Bennington regards education as a sensual and ethical, no less than an intellectual process. It seeks to liberate and nurture the individuality, the creative intelligence, and the ethical and aesthetic sensibility of its students, to the end that their richly varied natural endowments will be directed toward self-fulfillment and toward constructive social purposes. We believe that these educational goals are best served by demanding of our students active participation in the planning of their programs, and in the regulation of their own lives on campus. Student freedom is not the absence of restraint, however; it is rather the fullest possible substitution of habits of self-restraint for restraint imposed by others. The exercise of student freedom is the very condition of free citizens, dedicated to civilized values and capable of creative and constructive membership in modern society.

Brave words, but Bennington has taken them literally and rebuilt itself around them. Among the "first principles" adopted by the board is that the college be "student-centered" rather than "instruction-centered."

Bennington should help its students compose 600 variations on a single major. That major is widely seen not as a set of subjects but as a set of capacities and dispositions. . . .

All liberal learning—from philosophy to physics to poetry to painting—should be taught as a performing art by teacher-practitioners who teach, in the words of one, what keeps them awake at night.

Intellectually rigorous dialogue around the act of making—whether it be artifacts, ideas, or experiments— will be the college's dominant pedagogic method and the source of its special intensity.

To ensure that the faculty be composed "entirely of teacher-practitioners"—and not without considerable hue, cry, and litigation—about a third of the teaching staff was replaced. The board abolished academic divisions (not to speak of departments), relying on faculty to teach their disciplines from within small ad hoc program groups "with overlapping interests in multifaceted subjects." Tenure has been replaced by a formal, flexible, multiyear contract system—with contracts ranging from short-term to lifetime—which, in reviewing faculty performance, gives at least equal emphasis to the quality of teaching: "Members of the faculty shall be teacher-practitioners who are makers of original work and whose work and teaching are in fruitful interaction."

In thinking through their individual majors, students are supported by continuous faculty advising and feedback. Writing is "an essential dimension" of the advising relationship. Each year, students write reflective essays on their educational experience. In the second year the student works with the adviser on the design of a curricular plan for the next three semesters. In the third year the student writes an evaluation of progress and proposes for approval a plan for the fourth year. The student's revised plan for the fourth year is reviewed by a panel (six faculty members and the dean) which makes final recommendations.

Some of the guidelines for this process are so uniquely "Bennington" that they are worth special notice:

- Anything well and interestingly defended is possible.
- The questions: Who am I? What do I want? What do I need? are considered to be sincere, complicated and their pursuit essential.
- Students should be encouraged to make their own inquiry into: what is or ought an education to be? what should someone graduating from here have done—experienced—felt—accomplished? what *is* growth?

Experiences that should be incorporated in a Bennington education whatever the particulars of its design:

- Working to one's peak capacity in an area you love;
- Being changed/astonished;
- Taking responsibility (job/teaching etc.);
- Trying something new;
- Developing new interests, discovering new abilities;
- Being flamboyant, showing off, performing publicly;
- Being monastic, private, studious, silent;
- Being of public use, giving;
- Working collaboratively in a group.

Even if studies are primarily "within" one area they should include:

- Contact with physical reality (dissecting a pig, or at least examining something in such a way that one realizes that one hadn't seen it at all before);
- Reading of all kinds;
- Familiarity with the past;
- Capacity to research a topic;
- Engagement with a culture and a language other than one's own.

One of the few graduation requirements at Bennington is participation each year in a seven-week off-campus fieldwork term in which students take jobs or internships in areas that complement their studies "in fields ranging from publishing to politics, from arts administration to teaching, from medical research to social work." Students thus acquire work experience, with all the references, professional contacts, job-seeking skills, and self-confidence that come with it. They write summary papers on their fieldwork experience that are evaluated and become part of their college record.

For its size, Bennington has remarkable resources for instruction in the visual and performing arts and in creative writing, and a goodly number of its students concentrate their studies in those areas. But it is by no means an art school; rather, it is deeply committed to the arts as an essential component of education. As President Coleman has put it,

> At Bennington, over time, the arts have tended to transform the energy of the more traditional academic disciplines, bringing to the culture of the college a kind of life that does not run out of steam, accompanied by a resistance to trendiness. The charms of following and submitting to the crowd are no match for the consuming intensity of immersion in a craft, a discipline; the challenge of engaging in the as-yet untried; the courage it takes to think independently.

> To use the arts and practicing artists to help transform education into something more active, more collaborative, more penetrating will take a revolution in the way we think about teaching. It means providing alternative models to that of the student as passive recipient of received truths, predigested ideals of beauty, distant and disembodied images of excellence. In the new model, the idea of the studio replaces the lecture hall; the role of the teacher approaches that of master to apprentice, coach to athlete, and, eventually, of colleague to colleague; and the student's own work becomes the grounds for evaluating accomplishment, rather than the capacity to reiterate the work of the teacher.

Steven J. Tepper has recently proposed five key "structural conditions" in colleges "that foster creativity":

1. Creativity thrives within teams and collaborative circles;
2. Creativity flourishes in diverse environments where there are adequate opportunities for cross-cultural exchange;
3. Creativity is stimulated by interdisciplinary exchange;
4. Creative people need time to develop their ideas, test their hypotheses and prepare to recognize the big idea when it comes;
5. Creativity requires an environment that tolerates and even encourages failure.

He then argues that, in addition, "the arts have long been recognized as important catalysts for creative work across domains. . . . the arts attract more talented students in every discipline and create a more stimulating place to work and study." On the basis of these principles, Bennington has become what must be one of the most creative campuses in the country.

Another conspicuously successful innovative design is that of Hampshire College. It opened in 1970, partly through the agency of the presidents of Amherst, Mount Holyoke, Smith College, and the University of Massachusetts at Amherst, and it benefits greatly from its proximity to these schools, since students may take courses in all. Hampshire has no departments, but it does have five interdisciplinary schools: Cognitive Science; Natural Science; Social Science; Humanities, Arts, and Cultural Studies; and Interdisciplinary Arts.

The program is divided into three divisions: the first year of "basic studies" includes a small beginning tutorial taught by the student's adviser, and a group of "highly specific, experiential courses buttressed by substantial project work" in each of the schools. Having become acquainted with Hampshire's collaborative and interdisciplinary learning style, students then prepare a portfolio of their work, including a self-evaluative essay, which is the basis for a third semester that includes planning with faculty advisers for the second division. The next three semesters (the second division) involve a coherent group of learning activities that make up the student's concentration, which is chosen with the approval of a faculty committee chaired by the adviser and may be changed in progress:

> A concentration . . . builds from work at foundational levels to advanced work. In the concentration, the student seeks to achieve a grasp of particular knowledge and techniques, the broader concepts that lie behind them, and critical and analytical skills appropriate to the relevant disciplines. A concentration may range from a plan of studies similar to that of a traditional college major to a highly individualized program of study. Its scope may be broad or narrow. It may include a number of different kinds of learning activities: independent studies and projects, courses, reading programs, internships, and other forms of field study.

In this division students are also expected to range freely outside their fields of concentration and to complete requirements in community service and "multiple cultural perspectives." The latter, spelled out in unusual detail, calls for work addressing at least one of two critical issues—Non-Western Perspectives, and Race in the United States—and including a third issue, Knowledge and Power:

> The influence of discrepancies in power and privilege is hidden from most scholarly discourse, where the canons of academic disciplines are apt to be presented as neutral and universal. Study of how academic knowledge may be shaped by relations of power and difference will help our students think more critically about the processes under which intellectual or artistic perspectives can be either privileged or marginalized. To achieve this goal, students must incorporate study of the relations between power and knowledge, in regard to either A (non-Western perspectives), or B (race), into their Division II.

A portfolio of all the course papers, evaluations, artistic works, reflective essays, or other evidence of what has happened in this division forms the basis for a final meeting with the committee, which passes on the work and submits a formal evaluation of it.

The third division, in the final year, is principally devoted to an "advanced independent study project," again approved, overseen, and evaluated by a committee including the adviser. The project, which grows out of the concentration, is accompanied by two further exercises of the student's "advanced" status, such as an advanced-level course, a supervised teaching activity, a supervised internship, or a course of independent study.

Hampshire students work within a framework of rules that are precisely defined, yet those rules are designed to foster the exercise of extraordinary personal freedom—along with personal responsibility. Students produce a marvelously varied array of concentrations and study projects, which, while highly "liberal" in their educational goals, are also highly instrumental in the transition to future occupations.

No account of innovation in college education would be complete without mention of Empire State College of the State University of New York. Empire State College provides for adults of a wide range of ages and conditions, with jobs, families, and diverse histories, usually enrolled part-time and unable to attend a conventional college. The college, in many respects, comes to them. It was founded in 1971—under the enlightened presidency of James W. Hall and the SUNY chancellorship of Ernest L. Boyer—and now serves some 16,000 students from a Center for Distance Learning and from thirty-five teaching locations in the state.

At Empire State, by the very nature of the situation, the student comes first. The college offers its A.A. and B.A. degrees in conventional academic majors and in interdisciplinary studies answering to almost any intellectually respectable objective that a student might come up with. Each degree program conforms to SUNY's general education requirements, but otherwise it is designed individually. Students engage in their programs each term through learning contracts—written agreements that specify the topics to be studied, the modes of learning to be used, the amount and level of credit to be assigned, and the terms for evaluating the work. Students are expected to take part in the design of their contracts and to become more and more deeply involved in conceptualizing their education and its goals as they progress. Assessment, including student self-assessment, is central to the whole process, and the college takes great pains, given the variety of students and their programs, to make it generous, rigorous, and fair.

The key to this unique curriculum is the role of the faculty. Faculty have the conventional academic qualifications of faculty elsewhere, but they have much deeper responsibility. At Empire State they are called "mentors." Mentoring may be described as teaching and advising combined, but raised to a higher level. Each student in the college has a mentor, and the two work together from orientation to graduation. They have frequent meetings in one of the many mentors' offices situated all over the state. The mentor collaborates with the student in designing contracts: choosing topics for study that will fit with the student's previous knowledge and experience as well as with his or her goals; considering the range of learning modes available (for instance, guided independent study with mentor or tutor, small study groups, Web-based distance-learning courses, residencies in special programs, internships in local organizations, cross-enrollment at other colleges); judging the amount and level of credit; and establishing criteria for evaluation. Subject to review by the college, the mentor is also responsible for evaluating the work and describing its outcome for the record. In addition to periodic meetings and discussions on progress and planning, the student may also meet with the mentor for formal study sessions.

In this situation, the mentor is not merely the conventional college adviser, who usually counsels to "get the requirements out of the way" and may then discuss a few possible majors and their prerequisites. At Empire State the mentor is continuously engaged with the student's education and must become acquainted with any part of his or her history and aspirations that may be relevant to it; the mentor must lead, or rather accompany, the student to a goal that often turns out to be different or wider or deeper than the one first envisioned. Experienced and expert practitioners report that ideally what the two of them do is engage in an extended dialogue, in which the mentor is a learner as well as a teacher.

Mentoring thus requires personal academic expertise coupled with unusual interdisciplinary range; it entails a gradual but continuous enlargement of the mentor's intellectual scope to answer to each student's needs and experiences. It also requires an intimate knowledge of the college's resources, both known formal offerings and the various capacities of colleagues. In carrying out this planning, study, and assessing, mentors must be able to judge when the topic is out of their own range, so that others with the right professional competence can be brought in.

Teaching older adults has obvious differences from teaching conventional college students. The former are a much more varied crew and have substantial life experience and better-defined objectives. They require a different educational stance on the part of the college and its faculty. Still, Empire State has profound, innovative things to teach other colleges. The new curriculum would flourish anywhere that students were so unambiguously put first and the nature of education made a preoccupation of all. Other colleges could not do better than Empire State does: hire only teachers who are both intellectually broad and warmly sympathetic toward dialogue with students.

Since it opened in 1971, the Evergreen State College has won a reputation for being among the most hopeful and most important examples of the new curriculum in the nation. An independent campus in the State of Washington system, it is completely innovative and highly integrated. It serves the surrounding communities—79 percent of its 4,400 students are in-state residents—and is in no way dependent on the selection of an elite student body. Admittedly, the design and preservation of a state college campus of this sort has to be something of a miracle. Evergreen was favored from the first by progressive-minded founders and an experimentally oriented faculty, who were given a mandate to reform the curriculum and came up with a new but coherent plan. The six-year presidency of a popular former governor, Daniel J. Evans, beginning in the late 1970s, helped the college survive in the face of repeated political attempts to shut it down. The college grew, remained philosophically coherent while adapting itself to change, and has become an important influence on educational thinking across the nation.

Because the tradition of the college includes an unusually rigorous honesty of public expression—which must, incidentally, be a powerful teaching device—one can gather a surprisingly realistic picture of it from its official announcements. Here is the college's mission statement:

MAKING LEARNING HAPPEN

The Evergreen State College is a public, liberal arts college serving Washington State. Its mission is to help students realize their potential through innovative, interdisciplinary educational programs in the arts, social sciences, humanities, and natural sciences. In addition to preparing students within their academic fields, Evergreen provides graduates with the fundamental skills to communicate, to solve problems, and to work collaboratively and independently in addressing real issues and problems.

The principles "that guide the development of all college programs and services" are as follows: Teaching is the central work of the faculty at both the undergraduate and graduate levels. Supporting student learning engages everyone at Evergreen— faculty and staff.

Evergreen has virtually no formal requirements except for the 180 quarter units of credit needed to graduate, but it is consistent and emphatic on what it expects from students. Graduates must be able to assume responsibility for their work, participate collaboratively, communicate effectively, develop the ability "to appreciate and critically evaluate a range of problems, across academic disciplines," apply the proper modes of inquiry to these problems, and, in culmination, "demonstrate depth, breadth, and synthesis of learning and the ability to reflect on the personal and social significance of that learning." Long-term student capabilities, then, are the nucleus of the curriculum.

The faculty spends a great deal of thought and energy on planning the curriculum, which is remarkably fluid from year to year. There are no conventional academic departments; for curricular purposes the faculty is organized into "planning units," formed by affinity of interests. A group of fifteen or more faculty having the requisite focus and breadth of interdisciplinary learning may arrange to form a planning unit. Currently there are five: Culture, Text, and Language; Expressive Arts; Environmental Studies; Scientific Inquiry; and Social Science. There is an annual design and planning retreat. Each unit generates a group of offerings designed to give students "a strong background in the concepts, evidence and methods" in its own area, which is not a major but does provide a range of specializations. Representatives of each unit also collaborate with the others to design and staff more broadly interdisciplinary programs involving two or more areas and "core" programs, aimed at first-year entering students, providing orientation to the college and training in basic college skills.

Offerings are planned for three levels—beginning, intermediate, and advanced—and may take the form of coordinated studies, group contracts (with one or two faculty and 25 to 50 students studying a single topic at an intermediate or advanced level), and individual contracts (negotiated between a student and a faculty sponsor). Any of these can be used to generate academically related off-campus student internships.

As students progress, an increasing number engage in contract learning and internships. Students may also take single course offerings designed to ensure breadth in sometimes-neglected areas. But the primary teaching mode at Evergreen is the coordinated studies programs.

A coordinated studies program is a team-taught, generally full-time (16 credits per quarter), interdisciplinary unit with two to five faculty and forty-eight to one hundred students. The work is centered around a common reading list, seminar discussions, lectures, workshops, individual projects and sometimes internships. The programs often run the full academic year (48 credits) and require full-time work (40+ hours) from students. Each faculty member on the team contributes to the common work, which is usually organized around a theme or problem to be examined from a variety of academic disciplines.

Coordinated studies programs are available for all student levels.

Each teaching team formed to offer one of these programs has authority over the whole program, including class hours; the team also meets in its own faculty seminar, and faculty who are not currently in programs are nevertheless expected to join existing teams or form their own seminars. The collaborative, interdisciplinary study performed by the seminars is considered an important scholarly activity; it regularly produces ideas and materials that are later brought into the curriculum.

Here is an example of a coordinated studies program recently offered for freshmen.

Interrogating American Cultures through the Arts, a core course offered by three faculty members for three quarters, and described as follows:

This program will examine the multiplicity of cultures in North America made up of both the indigenous peoples and the settlers from around the world and will interrogate the notion of "American culture." This study will also include issues of cultural hybridity and intercultural interaction and will involve the exploration of these topics through the study of history, literature, art history, visual arts, film, multimedia and dance theater.

Students will focus on individual communities through

readings, discussions, reflective writing and hands-on projects. They will reflect on their selves and own ethnic identity, as well as influences from growing up in a diverse society, dealing with issues of identity, cultural hybridity and insider/outsider dynamics.

In winter, there will be research writing about cultures that have shaped the vitality of the American scene: Native American, South Asian American, Irish American, Japanese American, Armenian American, Appalachian, Chinese American, Mexican American and African American, as well as those of mixed cultural heritage. All students will be expected to participate in hands-on workshops in Orissi dance, mixed media art and/or multimedia production and to produce creative as well as written work on the themes of the program. They will also begin working towards multimedia performances.

In spring, students' multimedia, interactive performances and/or installations will be performed and shown on and off campus, in the community and in public schools.

Students will interact with visual artists, performing artists, media artists and Evergreen alumni in the arts. There will be field trips to cultural events in Seattle and Native American communities. (Credit awarded in multicultural American history, visual arts, media studies, Orissi dance, theater, cultural studies, English composition and American studies.)

Additional examples, the first being a course for intermediate students and the rest "all-level" courses, which make special provisions for beginning students, are

- Science of Mind, taught by three faculty members for three quarters;
- The Physicist's World, taught by two faculty members for two quarters;
- Belief and Truth, offered by two faculty members for one quarter;

- Public Works: Democracy and Design, offered by two faculty members for two quarters;
- Asian Culture and Art, offered by four faculty members for three quarters.

Full descriptions of these courses are given in the appendix.

Students plan their own courses of study at Evergreen and frequently contribute to shaping proposed new programs, suggesting projects, books, and guest lecturers. They are advised by faculty in their current programs. The programs—being full-time—are sustained and intensive enough for faculty to become extremely well acquainted with their students, who perform frequently in small-group seminars and do extensive writing. Since the programs taken by the student are each analyzed and recorded in terms of the fields and disciplines they engage, the faculty adviser can readily judge the breadth, quality, and coherence of each student's previous academic experience. At the end of a program, the student confers one-on-one with the adviser, who supplies a written evaluation of the student's progress. The students, as part of learning to reflect upon and articulate their own experience, evaluate their teachers and prepare self-evaluations after each program. Needless to say, letter grades are not used at Evergreen.

Team teaching is expected of every faculty member, and most prefer it. The constant, close intellectual engagement among its members makes it possible for the faculty to have an extraordinarily intimate knowledge of each other's scholarship and teaching ability. This has profoundly beneficial consequences for faculty appointment and retention. Before initially hiring regular faculty, great care is taken that candidates have

1. Previous experience or clearly expressed desire to participate in collaborative, interdisciplinary teaching;
2. A willingness to work as a member of a coordinated studies team;
3. Demonstrated expertise in one or more fields of study and a willingness to participate with students in learning new

fields (a Ph.D. is not in itself a requirement for hiring or retention);

4. A willingness to teach and learn through the exploratory, cooperative seminar mode;
5. A willingness to work with students in tutorials and individual contracts;
6. A willingness to act as an academic advisor;
7. A willingness to participate in TESC governance activities, including DTFs. [DTFs, or Disappearing Task Forces, Evergreen's answer to faculty committees, deal with major policy issues and disband when their work is done.]

Applicants submit student evaluations and a written account of their educational philosophy, and as part of their campus interview they teach a class and present their own design for an ideal team-taught program.

To reduce competition and promote collaboration, there are no professorial ranks or competitive salaries at Evergreen. Having survived the college's stringent appointment procedure and a major review after three to six probationary years of teaching, a faculty member is presumed to have the right to continuing appointment; nonreappointment is uncommon. However, tenured faculty participate in a salutary formal review every five years. For this review, each member maintains a substantial portfolio including, among other things, all program syllabi and an annual self-evaluation addressing published criteria for good teaching, meeting commitments, planning curricula, participating in college affairs, and developing professionally. In addition, the portfolio contains not only all evaluations by the faculty member of other Evergreen faculty and of students but also all evaluations of the faculty member by other faculty and by students, along with the students' evaluations of themselves. The faculty member also submits a retrospective five-year self-evaluation and a prospective three-year teaching and learning plan.

This detailed record is then reviewed by a panel consisting of the dean and all the available colleagues with whom the member has taught in the past five years. Meeting with the panel, the member receives notice of and praise for his or her best work, suggestions for improvement of less successful work, and encouragement and comments about plans for self-development and for future teaching. Given the richness of the information and the intimacy of available judgment involved, reviews are extraordinarily deep and reliable, and regular faculty are commonly reappointed.

Evergreen was studied by the National Survey of Student Engagement as one of the twenty "strong-performing" colleges and universities in its DEEP (Documenting Effective Educational Practice) project. The colleges were examined over a period of two years to determine what factors contribute to student success. The final report on the Evergreen case study puts Evergreen students in the very highest percentiles of college students for active and collaborative learning and is in general highly commendatory:

> Owing to its founding ideals and values, the College's academic and management structures and operating philosophy are unusual compared with most state-supported colleges and universities. There is an absence of competition, status, cliques, and overall imperiousness that too often characterizes an institution of higher education. Evergreen is also marked by collaboration, an unusual and functional kind of egalitarianism, and a special level of caring and community. As one person put it, "there is a conviction that we are providing a powerful learning environment," which is manifested as a love for academic work that pervades the place. . . .

> The faculty is deeply committed to the liberal arts, to teaching, to working collegially in an interdisciplinary mode, and to the academic values and processes that are distinctive and central to Evergreen. They are also intellectually alive, vital, and have a visible dedication to

learning—something that, once again, is fueled by the form and substance of Evergreen's special curricular approach. The College is not organized into traditional academic departments. Faculty members believe strongly that the traditional departmental organization inevitably results in narrowness of intellectual view, and departmental politics, and promotional and appointment rituals that consume time and energy that could be better spent with educational matters. (11)

Evergreen is by no means without its problems. Although its student body is highly self-selected (with a high proportion of transfer students), its insistence on self-motivation means that some students fail for lack of enough structure. Its avoidance of formal requirements means that uniform assessment of student achievement in such skills as writing, critical thinking, and quantitative reasoning is difficult. In the present environment of stingy public support for colleges, faculty and staff are seriously underpaid. The college's 2003 accreditation report noted,

The problem of underfunding extends beyond salary alone. . . . Faculty already carry a heavy load of instruction with high expectations regarding interaction with individual students; in addition they have a near constant requirement for planning instructional programs (year long and shorter instructional programs for two years hence) in teams with fellow faculty often requiring significant time commitments during the summer; they also participate pervasively in campus governance and policy development.

The combination leaves little time during the academic year and even summers for continuing personal professional development to maintain competence and currency in their fields and to engage in scholarship. In that context the reduction in the number of sabbaticals available becomes significant for a campus seeking academic excellence in teaching.

Despite these and other difficulties, which the college is alertly addressing, Evergreen remains attractive to prospective faculty. As the DEEP report puts it,

> In the present era of a narrow, often suffocating focus on prestige and research epitomized by the research universities, one might think it would be difficult to recruit faculty who are committed to investing themselves fully in careers of teaching. This is an especially important question as the last of the founding faculty near retirement. Can equally dedicated and effective replacements be found? Evergreen's recent searches have resoundingly answered that question in the affirmative. There are ample numbers of scholars who seek situations like those offered by Evergreen where one can be invested fully in interdisciplinary teaching, unencumbered by the politics and narrowness of departments. (12)

Evergreen is not the only college with high ideals, nor does it represent the only way to bring about constructive innovation. But it demonstrates what is still possible for innovative public education.

Research, Scholarship, Teaching, and the Education of Professors

Reform of American college education will come about in line with some of the ideas and models presented in the previous chapters. Though the ideas have been out there for decades, and the existence of a few truly innovative colleges most hopeful, on a national scale our progress has been very slow. We will not by any means get substantial educational reform until we confront the faculties themselves.

It is an amazing paradox that the faculties that have profited from advances in research in all other fields of learning have generally failed to do so in their own backyard. In the past century, research in departments of education did not enjoy much prestige elsewhere in the academy. Much of the work was plodding or worse, and the writing generally execrable. On the rare occasions when educational research was noticed, it was usually to be criticized; a few members of the mainline research establishment made second careers out of castigating scholarship in education. Today, however, the quality of the work is much improved, and some scholars of higher education enjoy reputations as great as any in social science; yet other faculties are still mainly ignorant of this work.

Your typical professor is hardly aware of new thinking in education, does not read educational periodicals, and rarely goes beyond the academic department in discussing problems of teaching and learning. The dominant idea is that professors deal with subject matter; "education" is for high-school teachers.

Furthermore, innovation costs money, and anything that might compete with funds for research is suspect at best. Unconventional studies, especially interdisciplinary ones, that suggest that someone might have the audacity to investigate and teach something in which he or she is not a certified expert still seem to some professors to be advocating a relaxation of "our" standards, which are of course "rigorous" in the extreme. It is clear that the religion of "research" with its cult of expertise is one of the principal obstacles to the improvement of college education.

"RESEARCH" AND "SCHOLARSHIP"

I do not mean to belittle research itself. The capacity for research, for the discovery of new knowledge, most clearly exemplified in science, medicine, and technology, is one of our most precious resources; if its results do not—in the wrong hands—lead finally to the demise of civilization, they are surely essential to preserving it. One need only think of recent advances in biochemistry or of the intellectual reach of modern astrophysics to be convinced of the overwhelming importance and beauty of research. We need research. Indeed, we need more good research and more funding for it.

However, it is precisely this importance, and the rewards that go with it, that have made research such a detriment to undergraduate education. Our colleges were originally founded to educate students. But since the creation in 1876 of Johns Hopkins, our first research university, and especially since World War II, research has occupied a larger and larger proportion of the energy of college faculties.

The unchallengeable reason for this is that the scientific and technical expertise of faculties is of immense value to the community; it is entirely proper that colleges and universities, public ones in particular, render this service and be applauded for it. What is damaging, however, is that the research establishment has at the same time acquired grossly unwarranted power over the education of students. In recent years the research record has virtually replaced the capacity for teaching as a criterion for becoming a professor and as a measure of its rewards. When departments look at young scholars for appointment or promotion, the first (and often the only) question always is, How about the research? As a result, educational organization and curricula are heavily controlled by the research mentality, and many talented people with a desire to teach but not to do research are driven to the margins of the profession, or, unwilling to subsist on second-class pay and status, out of it altogether.

Two widespread notions that perpetuate the dominance of research over teaching, and mask its damaging effects on education, are that research and teaching are in fact inextricably related, and that being a researcher makes one a better teacher.

Reexamining these notions deserves special care, and first off we will need clear definitions, especially of the terms "research" and "scholarship." The whole question has been most notably discussed by Ernest L. Boyer in *Scholarship Reconsidered: Priorities of the Professoriate.* I am greatly indebted to Boyer in the present discussion. But Boyer embraces the entire scope of professorial activity under the term "scholarship," which he divides into four categories: "scholarship of discovery" (original research), "scholarship of integration" (criticism and interpretation), "scholarship of application" (service), and "scholarship of teaching." Several colleges have already adopted Boyer's definitions in liberalizing their criteria for faculty tenure. I do not adopt his terminology, however, because I feel that "scholarship of teaching" is ambiguous (scholarship done by teachers? scholarship about teaching?). Additionally, putting it under the same tent with "scholarship of discovery" has the appearance of trying to appropriate for teaching the prestige of research, thus reinforcing the research religion rather than examining critically the proper differences between scholarship and research.

"Research" ought to refer to the pursuit and discovery of new knowledge. "Original research" should include not only discovering new facts and phenomena but also finding new, meaningful relationships among them. Original criticism, new interpretation, fresh insight, answering the questions Why? and

How? is the "research" typically done in the humanities and social studies.

Although the borders cannot be clearly drawn, "research" in these senses occupies a special domain *within* the far wider activity that I call "scholarship." This is the activity that should characterize the lifetimes of all good teachers as they acquire the learning that qualifies them for the teaching profession. It is obvious that good scholarship should include the engagement with complex ideas and an imaginative, creative approach to problems. Nevertheless, much of the learning acquired in the course of teaching must itself be the product of someone else's original "research"; this is the only sense in which research and teaching are inextricable. One obviously cannot be a great teacher without being a scholar, that is, without asking the important questions and studying the results of research; but one need not have published original research oneself.

Indeed, many college teachers have never published research, and many do not particularly want to. Original research is a rather rare skill, and relatively few people have the requisite disposition, knowledge, imagination, and persistence to bring it off. It is also a calling, a passion, and an art; and it is not only emotionally consuming to its best practitioners but famously time-consuming and often solitary as well. Just as you can't keep a true writer from writing, you can't keep a true researcher from researching. It follows that researchers want to devote the required inordinate amounts of their time to *doing* research. Anything else, including teaching, is a distraction.

Teaching is also and equally a calling and an art, and professors whose talents lead them to think of themselves essentially as teachers eagerly pursue scholarship but do not undertake research with primary enthusiasm. Teachers deal massively with knowledge and insight, but they deal with it primarily in relation to students. Their first love is teaching students, not doing research. Not only does research take time from teaching and scholarship, it is almost inescapably narrowing. To do original research in most fields today, to be "on the cutting edge," is to be a specialist, is to have severely narrowed your focus. It is well recognized that even professors in the same academic department are often mutually incomprehensible as far as their current research goes. As for undergraduate teaching, the last thing you want is narrowness. Most good teachers are good teachers partly because they are good scholars, that is, people who teach in the areas in which they are most deeply engaged, and who are continuingly and progressively learned in the areas they teach. But even if they necessarily have special areas of interest, they typically pursue breadth and clarity. Attempting to help their students make sense of the world, they persistently try to make sense of the world for themselves. In the course of a lifetime of study, they may occasionally come upon ideas or insights that are so original as to warrant publishing an article or book about them. But their primary allegiance is to learning and teaching, not to research.

There is thus a vast area of learning that might not be characterized as "original research," might not be publishable in books or in journals, and yet is invaluable "scholarship" and indispensable to teaching. For whom, after all, are the original texts, the new facts and figures, and the new historical and social and scientific insights produced by research most fittingly intended if not for teachers? For what use are our great libraries, our incomparable resources of reference, unless ideally for that of teachers? For education, putting the world together—integrating the things that you are learning with the things that you know, making as coherent sense of your universe as you can—is arguably even more important than the distinctions and fractionations yielded by research. Other things being equal, I would rather have my grandchildren taught literature by a person with a lively grasp of the texts and richly furnished with their historical, literary, linguistic, and cultural background than by a person who had only published research on some narrow aspect of the field. And the same is analogously true in other fields, even in science.

It is true that in some fortunate lives original research arises

curse that does incalculable inner damage to many college teachers and hobbles the development of their scholarly capacities as well.

Both of the alternatives are equally damaging: Where the research impulse dominates, it inevitably comes at the expense of the student. I still remember with pain the courses wasted for me as an undergraduate by professors who simply "taught" their current narrow, technical researchings in place of wider materials. Many a graduate teaching assistant is at this very moment inflicting some form of his or her dissertation research on the unsuspecting, pitiful attentions of a freshman section. On the other hand, where teaching wins out over the research imperative—as we have already observed—the teacher suffers, by failing to receive tenure or by settling for other forms of second-class status.

The damage to higher education does not merely consist in what the research imperative has wrought upon teachers who are not researchers. The damage done by denying talented teachers entry to the profession or honor therein is probably exceeded by the educational pollution created when narrow research criteria are used for admitting and promoting the wrong people. A lot of them get in, and the resultant waste of time, money, and spirit could hardly be calculated.

The research concept has become so sanctified in academia that in faculty discussions of research and teaching it is seldom admitted that some people are good researchers but bad teachers. And why should some *not* be bad teachers? The desire to teach students is not necessarily the only motive behind becoming a professor. Some people have a temperamental thirst for discovery. Their minds are so curious and restless and powerful that they can scarcely keep themselves from research, and in what place better than a university or college? For others, the prestige, the lifestyle, and recently the money to be enjoyed by a good researcher are motives enough. Others come by a sort of inertia. They have always been good in school. They get good grades in high school and in college and go on to graduate school, where they get more good grades. Though they may have no particular aptitude for teaching, nor give a rap for undergraduates, the place itself is most congenial, and so they play the game, the name of which is research . . . and some teaching. If they have a touch of the authoritarian in their personality, they enjoy in turn the power to decide who gets good grades and who does not. If they are not dedicated teachers, people of this sort at best take up the space, time, funds, and students that might more suitably belong to good teachers, and however much their research may benefit the community and support the public reputation of the college, they lower the quality of its instruction.

Even less can be said for those who are not such good researchers either, but who, taking advantage of the almost criminal simplicity to which the research imperative has been reduced—PUBLISH!—succeed in giving the impression of being good researchers by being prolific publishers. In many, many cases quantity outweighs quality. Ernest Boyer, in *Scholarship Reconsidered* (table A-25), reports the results of a 1989 national survey of the opinions of over 5,000 faculty members from institutions of all kinds on the proposition "At my institution publications used for tenure are just counted, not qualitatively measured." Forty-two percent of faculty at "research" universities agreed, as did 53 percent at "doctorate-granting" and 54 percent at "comprehensive" schools. In some colleges, where administrators and faculties evidently feel themselves incompetent to judge their colleagues' research, a published article is given points depending on what journal it appeared in. It takes a certain number of points to get tenure.

The push to publish "original research," to find something that has not already been "done" by someone else, produces in mediocre hands work that is increasingly narrow, derivative, and unimportant. A very large proportion of researchers are followers of the bandwagon, picking over and mopping up after the main show has passed by. Judging what is or is not a bad piece of research is admittedly a professional matter, but I have no doubt that well over half, and probably more, of all published research is of questionable value to anyone but its author. If pushed, I would have to guess, after a lifetime of reading thousands of research proposals in a lot of different fields, that no more than 15 percent or so are conceivably worth the cost to society that they would entail. I recently asked two eminent physicists, one in theoretical, the other in experimental physics, what percentage of the research in their fields they thought worth the time and effort. Both answered, "5 percent."

There is substantial evidence in this direction from publishing statistics. The production of scholarly monographs has become so inflated—both in quantity and quality—that publishers, especially university presses, are increasingly unwilling to print them. Furthermore, scholars are increasingly unwilling to buy and read them.

Of course, a lot of research that appears trivial or arcane to the layperson, and that makes good sport for politicians and anti-intellectuals, may well be important enough to the learned community: *uninformed persons are not entitled to judge the value of research.* But by the same token the scholarly establishment should take this responsibility a lot more seriously than it does. There is a level at the very top, especially in science, where evaluation is unwaveringly rigorous. But most professors today tend to lean over backward to be tolerant of the "research" of their colleagues.

One view is that however trivial a piece of research looks now, who knows whether it may not in the future become valuable? An assortment of seemingly trivial details, patiently assembled, may well contribute later to someone else's big picture. There are certainly a few recorded cases of an investigator's unregarded research turning out to be a key piece in the great discovery by someone else, and it can be argued that *all* knowledge is somehow valuable. But the question is, or should be, Is even the *potential* value of such knowledge worth the expenditure of resources, not to mention of human lifetime, it has taken? More particularly, has it been worth it for the college, whose mission is to promote the learning of students?

There is surely much to be admired in the industry and single-mindedness of a whole class of antiquarians and studious hobbyists of every sort who widely populate academia and belong—as is their undeniable right—to a vast assortment of learned societies. But I have never heard a serious discussion of the problem that arises where the pursuit of uniquely personal scholarly goals (and personal pleasure) has a manifestly dim prospect for anyone else's enlightenment. At what point does "research" become pedantry? In the academy the question is hardly ever engaged.

Poor research is tolerated for other reasons. At least it is quantifiable, much more so than is teaching. And it gives a certain evidence of industry. One of the great, silent specters that haunt colleges—ever present to the imaginations of administrators and colleagues alike—is Sloth. It is perhaps an inheritance of the centuries before research was invented, in which university scholars acquired a reputation for being uniformly dissolute and lazy. In any case, research results, no matter how unimportant, are taken to be a proof of character. If academic tenure raises uncomfortable misgivings, "research" allays them.

But the question remains: Is the massive waste of time, money, and energy in poor research exacted by the imperative to publish *worth it* to the community? Or would it be better to devote those precious fiscal and human resources to the broad learning essential to good teaching?

THE RESEARCH MENTALITY AND THE IDEA OF TEACHING

The preferred status of research as an activity of professors is by no means the only factor in its dominance over teaching on campus. *The research mentality also deeply defines the notion of what teaching actually is, and what should be taught to students.* Small wonder that teaching and research are widely touted to be inextricably interdependent—"our people can do both"—where the very conception of good teaching centrally involves the transmission of expert information and the curriculum offers mainly the latest information of the experts. But in recent years it has become clearer and clearer that this is not the best model for either teaching or the curriculum. Expert information, multiplying at an ever-accelerating rate and just as rapidly becoming outdated, manifestly cannot be the central basis of an education, just as the magisterial stance, no matter how authoritative, cannot be the best basis for teaching.

Information is of course an essential human resource, and remembering it an essential human capacity. None of us could make a move without it. We all need a working supply at hand to get through the day and through our jobs. Judging from the popular taste for quiz shows, however, you would think that remembering facts was our sovereign mental power. But while there is no learning without subject matter, information is only a part, and not the most important part, of our intellectual equipment.

One great thing about information is that it can all be classified, stored, preserved indefinitely, and handily retrieved—lately better than ever. As our supply of it surges, and remembering more than a tiny fraction of it becomes virtually impossible, how much you can remember becomes less and less important than knowing what you need and how to find it. In any but the most elementary and mundane areas of self-preservation, remembering information is less powerful than investigative skills.

But the most valuable skills are those that go beyond information gathering into the realms of meaning and understanding. Here the central questions are not What? When? and Where? but How? and Why? An educated person is one who is able to autonomously bring knowledge to bear on explanation, on the solution of significant problems. While education goes on within a medium of information, without which it would come to a standstill, its central character is the growing of a permanent set of intellectual skills and grounding in the major modes of thought. Most university instruction involves, in addition to factual content, the establishment of the vocabularies and contexts proper to each field of knowledge, and, most importantly, the learning of theories, principles, and laws—from the semipermanent laws discovered by natural science to the more transient hypotheses of the social sciences, the arts, and the humanities.

This material, often of great explanatory power, gives college work much of its sophistication. But from an educational point of view, conventional college instruction even in contextual and theoretical matters falls short of the mark, for it is more often than not *handled as if it too were information:* material delivered to the student from above, to be received, memorized, and given back in much the same form as it was handed down by an expert. As Professor Jonathan Z. Smith has observed: "Despite the proud claim that we make over and over again that we teach the how rather than the what of the disciplines, we, in fact, do not; it is the theoretical conclusion that our students underline in their books. I spend half an hour with each of my students looking at what they've underlined, and they've always underlined the punch line and never anything that might be called the process that led up to it."

It is true that a few students, sufficiently imaginative even at this level of learning, manage to go on to become autonomous thinkers. But most do not, because the magisterial system has not placed them in a situation that expects and allows them to discover and apply ideas by themselves.

There is of course a huge disparity between the rhetoric of college catalogs and the actualities on the ground. This announcement of the aims of a well-regarded research university is typical: "Tufts' rigorous academic programs are designed to teach students to make decisions, think independently, solve problems, take intellectual risks, challenge conventional wisdom, communicate effectively and explore the latest knowledge and research in all fields."

This is all well and good, but little in the undergraduate program is specifically designed to fulfill these aims. The university's College of Liberal Arts does permit the election of an individual major or an "interdisciplinary" minor (consisting of five courses from at least three different departments and a senior project), but most of its students take the typical curriculum: a large array of academic majors; rather wider-than-usual course requirements in writing, foreign language, world civilizations, and quantitative reasoning; and "distribution" in five areas—arts, humanities, social science, natural science, and mathematical sciences. Oddly, though the university boasts a thirty-year-old experimental college, styled "a major locus for educational innovation," students are not permitted to take more than one of its courses in satisfaction of the ten-course distribution requirement.

Look at most college lists of undergraduate courses and degree requirements and you will find a similar situation. The courses are almost always too large, a smorgasbord collection of the world's subject matter, defined, divided, and controlled by academic departments. After a few elementary introductory courses of general scope, each department's courses quickly become specialized, often peculiarly so, depending on the power of the institution's faculty. The more powerful the faculty, the freer they are to follow their own propensities—that is, to teach in and around their current research projects. So college undergraduates usually have an ample choice of courses to take, but the courses are virtually all designed to transmit academically classified subject matter that is of primary interest to college professors but not necessarily to students nor even to citizens.

A great many college courses are graded by multiple-choice and true/false exams; they are by this token alone manifestly useful only to teach information. But the case is not that much better for courses that make use of essay quizzes and exams. Anyone who has deciphered the answers desperately played back in a pile of semiliterate final-exam blue books—even from seniors at highly rated institutions—knows how dispiriting the results can be. Where the material is *received to be memorized* rather than *discovered,* the inferior model of learning compromises the educational process from the first. The idea was long ago expressed by John Dewey in *Democracy and Education* (1916):

No thought, no idea, can possibly be conveyed as an idea from one person to another. When it is told, it is, to the one to whom it is told, another given fact, not an idea. The communication may stimulate the other person to realize the question for himself and to think out a like idea, or it may smother his intellectual interest and suppress his dawning effort at thought. But what he *directly* gets cannot be an idea. Only by wrestling with the conditions of the problem at first hand, seeking and finding his own way out, does he think.

The magisterial method of teaching has of course a distinguished history. It has generated an agelong tradition of the veneration of knowledge and of the learned. In cultures in which knowledge is limited and thought to be permanent, handing it down from master to student would seem to be the best method. In the modern European tradition, however, since the seventeenth century—beginning with thinkers of the stamp of Bacon, Descartes, Galileo, and Newton—both the limits and the permanence of knowledge have been progressively blurred. And now, by the twenty-first century, the capacity to navigate intellectually in a wide sea of changing ideas has become more valuable than memorizing anything. As I have already remarked, it is one of the most amazing paradoxes in higher education that the research faculties have not massively applied this idea to the design of undergraduate teaching. For professors are by and large the most obvious group among the rare individuals who in their own college careers, one way or another, have managed to find their way out from under the magisterial regime to a capacity for independent thought.

The magisterial method has an obvious political side, which should further temper its usefulness in a democratic society. An authoritarian method, it is ideally suited to the propagation of orthodoxy. Where faith, obedience, and long-standing tradition are the main guides to survival, the power and the teaching of the established authorities suffice, and the capacity for independent thought can even be a serious political liability for the student. But for the modern European tradition, in which the idea of political freedom has expanded at the same rate as that of intellectual freedom, the conception of the ideal citizen has been reshaped, from that of a subject indoctrinated to follow an inherited regime to that of an independently informed and responsible individual who collaborates with other citizens in their own government. Since it is the education of this individual that concerns us here, it is clear that the learning of essential skills and the major modes of thought in an environment of discovery should be the nucleus of each student's curriculum.

THE EDUCATION OF PROFESSORS

Most training for prospective college teachers is training for the Ph.D., that is, training for original research. But that is not the best education for college teachers. Nor does it necessarily attract and retain in the profession those whose priority is teaching students. To prepare teachers to teach, and prepare them for a scholarship that will support teaching first, we will have to change the design of the Ph.D., both in the preliminary course work and in the dissertation. Instead of ever-narrowing specialization of subject matter, the graduate curriculum should cultivate breadth and complexity over several disciplines. It should teach a sophisticated pedagogy, based on the best educational thinking and on close apprenticeship to master teachers. The monographic doctoral dissertation, answering only to the current mania for a book, for a work of "original research," should be put aside in favor of broad scholarship, complex thought, and powers of clear expression.

Graduate education differs widely enough among disciplines and universities to prevent a compendious view of it in brief. I shall be referring mostly to the "traditional" curriculum practiced in the social sciences and humanities and pursued by most prospective college professors. In the sciences and engineering, graduate education is somewhat better funded and much more collaborative, and student dissertations are often dependent on and conducted within current faculty research projects. Some science dissertations are typically not so much books as reports or articles. However, the critique of the narrow research orientation of the graduate curriculum applies, if anything, even more to these fields.

The Graduate Curriculum

Efforts to reconceive graduate education have been going on for some decades now, but so far without conspicuous success. The graduate school is the very lair of the research establishment, and it is not receptive to interlopers. The prestige of the Ph.D. is still great and jealously defended by its holders. There have been attempts to get around this by proposing alternative degrees, such as the doctor of arts, with an emphasis on pedagogy and with different dissertation requirements. In the early 1960s the Carnegie Foundation, endorsed by the major higher-education associations, began funding D.A. degree programs, which were ultimately offered by thirty-one institutions. But these were generally beaten off by the major graduate schools as "second-class degrees." By 1999 the number had dwindled to thirteen schools, none of them among the largest. The doctorate, it is asserted—with sublime disregard for the oldest, most prestigious doctorate of all, the M.D.—is inevitably a research degree: its monographic dissertation gives evidence of the power of original investigation and testifies, especially in the social sciences and humanities, to the scholar's capacity to conduct a sustained (that is, book-length) argument.

Recently there have been more and more misgivings about the Ph.D. as it is currently conceived, even among those who do not question the primacy of research. There is a very high level of attrition among doctoral students—35 to 50 percent, depending on the field—partly because graduate training takes too long, up to twelve years in some disciplines. Graduate work is grossly undersupported, and as a result our graduate schools—despite some movement toward unionization of graduate students and collective bargaining—are among the worst sweatshops in the nation. Under the color of teacher training, too many students have to spend years of their study time working as underpaid assistants, often in sections of big lecture courses taught by professors, where they learn precious little about teaching, or as part-time instructors with primary responsibility for courses for which they are similarly ill prepared, overworked, and underpaid.

An equal failure of the Ph.D. curriculum is its poor design, much of which comes from the nature of the dissertation, as we can infer from the large number of A.B.D.'s, students who complete all the other requirements but not this. I do not subscribe to the notion that students who fail to produce a dissertation do not have the stuff to be good college teachers. There are many highly intelligent, cultivated graduate students who love to study and learn, to think and discuss, who want to spend their lives teaching, but who are not disposed or not yet ready to write a book. Many of the brightest and most admirable people I have ever met are A.B.D.'s who have turned to careers as teachers outside the major colleges or in foundations, public agencies, and other venues where their idealism, scholarship, and pedagogical talents are put to powerful use.

Writing a dissertation does not necessarily testify to the qualities we need in college teachers. A good and valuable book should ideally arise from a fresh idea, supported by ample funds for investigation and plenty of time to think, to write, and to revise. It *should* take some years to bring off; it should be, after all, the product of a mature situation. It should testify to its author's intelligence, learning, imagination, judgment, and coherence of expression. But the typical dissertation does no such thing. Often the idea is the professor's, not the student's. It is not necessarily a fresh, important idea, but may just be something that "hasn't been done." The probability that it will be of trivial significance is very high. Even if the topic is important, it may be impossible to bring it off in a limited time. When the project is done as an arbitrary research assignment, not as the natural outgrowth of one's continuing intellectual life, the scholar may not necessarily be deeply interested in it. But it is required for the prized degree. Couple this with the graduate student's characteristic poverty, lack of time, and stunted personal life, and it is no wonder that the project can become agonizing, and after some years the student simply quits. Apart from the modest number of natural researchers who have their own ideas and who would produce good book-length dissertations whether the faculty was around or not, those who somehow manage to finish a dissertation can mainly be certified as being able to stick to a long, difficult, unpleasant job to the finish. But while scholarship is difficult, it should at the same time be a joy, not a burden; and while persistence with the unpleasant may be a virtue, it is not what one thinks of first as a qualification for prospective college teachers.

Nor is it desirable to force prospective teachers to turn out work that is dispirited and drudging and thus likely to be second-rate or worse. One of the most important traits of the dissertation—conspicuously omitted even in discussions of its reform—is its typical badness. A prominent criticism of graduate school by students is that mentoring by a research-oriented faculty is often weak. Most graduate advisers are interested in working with good fellow researchers on promising projects, but they are not very interested in working with students. They were not trained or hired to do dissertation advising, and mostly they don't like it.

The acceptance of some Ph.D. dissertations can only be explained as the result of a combined dogged persistence on the part of the student and neglect on the part of the director. It is hard, finally, to turn down students—often moneyless—who have given too many years of their young lives toiling in the department, or working as underpaid adjuncts in some other college. It is hard, too, for faculty to remain interested in such uninspired and protracted labors. Some approved dissertations are so poorly thought out, researched, and written as to suggest that they have hardly been read by their faculty directors, much less by the busy "outside" faculty members conventionally appointed to pass on them. These "successful" candidates—doctors of philosophy at last!—have not only been trained, as it were, to do shoddy work; if they find teaching jobs at all, they now find themselves at the starting line of a race to publish or perish in which they have a built-in disadvantage.

The Ph.D. dissertation as currently envisioned works well for the small number of students who are able and willing to give themselves to the high degree of specialization necessary for original research and who wish to make this kind of research a focus of their lives. For them it should certainly be kept as an option. For the rest, there are more respectable options.

Graduate education should recruit young scholars who love students, and center on the learning and skills needed to be a good college teacher: interdisciplinary breadth, sensitivity to issues, lucid thought, powers of clear expression, a sophisticated grasp of investigative technique, a serious engagement with pedagogy, and a capacity to collaborate with colleagues. This prescription would not be difficult for an open-minded graduate faculty to translate into curricular terms: two years of course work concluding with an oral examination focusing on knowledge of the field, and a year or two to submit a portfolio of writings—say three or four substantial essays—collectively demonstrating essential attributes and skills.

The course work for the doctorate would involve substantial disciplinary coherence, enough to establish the candidate's preliminary competence to deal with a respectable field of learning. This, if anywhere, is the place in the curriculum for an academic "major." But the major should be broadly conceived and should require graduate course work in one or more other disciplines. Indeed, a goodly number of graduate departments have made progress in this direction at least. Claremont Graduate University requires a "transdisciplinary" course of all doctoral candidates. Wayne State offers a master of interdisciplinary studies degree. Vanderbilt University's Center for the Americas enables faculty and students from various disciplines to gather easily in informal groups, or in regular research groups, or in groups engaged in long-term projects. In 2006 the Yale School of Management instituted an exemplary M.B.A. curriculum based on new multidisciplinary courses.

This kind of graduate multidisciplinary study is often designed to support the candidate's engagement with the real-life problems that might be encountered in a professional career. But it would also provide ideal topics for future teaching projects. It is clear that a commitment to problematics need not in any way interfere with a commitment to sound scholarship. Scholars who may not be specializing in a given field must nevertheless be able to navigate in it. Continually studying, they must have a reliable control of the investigative techniques proper to whatever field they need to enter.

The two years of course work would also include substantial time spent in apprenticeships in the teaching of an undergraduate nuclear seminar and the planning of a large undergraduate planetary course, along with formal study and collegial discussion of the problems of each.

The portfolio of writings constituting the final stage of the doctorate could be just as respectable as the current dissertation is and a more precise indicator of the candidate's powers. Some of these powers might well be specified in advance, as part of the portfolio's definition. Thus one essay might emphasize research technique. Another might require dealing with an interdisciplinary problem. One essay might have to deal with education or course design. All would demonstrate the ability to write clearly. Some essays would naturally have arisen out of course work and then been expanded and revised; others would be new, generated out of the interplay of the candidate's most recent ideas. Together, they would be coherently, if broadly, related. All would point toward future study and thought.

Demonstrating thus the scope and depth of the candidate's mind, the portfolio would be ideal for use in securing a teaching position. It would surely be a lot more rewarding for prospective colleagues to read than the average dissertation.

The Graduate Department

It is an incontestable fact that graduate education does not prepare the majority of students for the careers or places in which they ultimately find themselves. They are trained to do research, but most will spend their lives teaching undergraduates or leave the academy for other careers. Nevertheless, remaking the graduate departments in the interest of their students will be even more difficult than remaking the undergraduate departments. The power and prestige of research faculty on the graduate level is almost absolute, and here they would seem to be on impregnable turf. The graduate departments *are* par excellence the natural location for training in research.

Segregating research faculty in well-financed institutes might clear the scene for serious reform of the undergraduate curricula. One could imagine a college or university in which research is administratively located in one or more institutes, which would also be responsible for graduate training in research. The members of the institutes, who might be specially titled "the research professor of ——," would work full-time in the institutes on research during their tenure, which might be for fixed periods or for life. They would teach, when they taught at all, mainly graduate students training for careers as researchers and would prescribe the curriculum for such students. They would be appointed to membership in the institute by peer review. The college or university would determine who constituted the body of peers, whether institute members only, members of the faculty body outside the institute, or experts from afar. The institute's activities would be funded as at present. The number of professors formally charged with conducting research would be considerably decreased by this change; accordingly, research support for each should be considerably larger. Members of the research institutes would not per se have jurisdiction or responsibility for undergraduate education on campus. That would be the province of the "teaching" faculty, who might be titled, as at present, "professor of ——."

But there are good arguments for keeping some top researchers in possible contact with all graduate students; they still have much to offer scholars headed for college teaching. The almost insurmountable problem would be to get them to accept the idea that training researchers is not the only and—from the public point of view—not the most important function of the graduate school. It would take considerable education, or pressure, to get this across.

If the graduate faculty is not to be formally divided, at the very least it should provide multiple curricula clearly defined by student purposes. Considering societal needs and the present mediocrity of academic research in general, the graduate schools should be spending two or three times as much effort on preparing college teachers as on preparing researchers. The proportion of students trained for research careers would be lessened but strengthened; only those with the rare and peculiar talents necessary for first-rate research would be permitted to risk that narrow path. The graduate faculty could be assembled by professional commitment in the same way: a small cadre of top researchers generously supported in institutes; another group who also spend some of their time in graduate instruction; and a cadre of top undergraduate teachers at the stage of their scholarly careers when they have something to offer graduate disciplinary or interdisciplinary instruction and can also mentor graduate students in the techniques of teaching.

Final Problems

ACCESS AND RETENTION

Paying primary attention to the curriculum should not allow us to pass over the fact that there are lots of other things about the American college that need improvement. One of our most urgent problems is that of access and retention, of finding and keeping places in college for students from poor families and for those who are potentially capable but are underprepared or lack motivation. Currently, only 52.6 percent of full-time students entering four-year public colleges graduate in six years; Hispanic students have a 41.8 percent rate, and African American students a 38.1 percent rate. The push toward ever greater selectivity at "elite" colleges, the scarcity of need-based scholarships, and the use of standardized entrance examinations on which children of lower-income families are less likely to succeed have meant that the gap in college going by income is actually widening. Almost all the increase in the proportion of eighteen- to twenty-four-year-olds in postsecondary institutions in recent years represents children from middle- and upper-income families.

While many agencies and colleges are addressing this problem with outreach and scholarship plans, it is ironic that most of them are laboring to recruit disadvantaged students into a second-rate system. Instead of sensitively introducing these students to the fascinating, unfamiliar culture of higher learning, the college courses prescribed for many of them typically have the same traits, often worsened by the label "remedial," that make them deadly for the regular student as well: bald presentations of subject matter in large, impersonal classes taught by overworked and underpaid part-timers, with emphasis on memory work for letter grades. These students deserve a first-rate curriculum, and it should be obvious that one based on close advising, small-group interaction, focus on interesting problems, and sensitive assessment would attract and retain more of them than the conventional one does.

In a sense, not only the disadvantaged but also most of our entering college students are underprepared. One of the reasons may be that high school teachers and administrators largely envision college preparation as preparation for the same mediocre curriculum that they themselves experienced. Future teachers and administrators, among all the students in college, are the ones who not only take the curriculum but also duplicate or perpetuate it. For other students, the college experience might be a means to an end; for future teachers it becomes an end and a model. Even if they start their careers teaching kindergarten, college remains a permanent presence in their professional lives. This is true both for the content of the curriculum and for the mode of teaching. So the curriculum has a greater resonance, has far greater consequences, mediated through the lives and experiences of future teachers than it has through the lives of ordinary students. That means that a poor college curriculum experienced by high school teachers will be poor for high school students too. As the Education Trust has reported: "Most of the problems that characterize secondary education in this country—unclear and differential standards, uneven teaching, little curricular coherence—can be found in spades in higher education as well. Indeed, these two systems are intertwined in so many places that neither can solve its own problems without the other's cooperation."

There are exceptions, of course, but they should not be allowed to obscure the general picture. Most of our high school teachers—for all their admirable idealism—have themselves gone though an experience in college that had no describable structure. They have come out of it with little more than a random collection of 120 semester units, including a "major" set in a miscellany of electives and "core" courses. The major probably consisted of a fixed number of courses in one department, not necessarily offering basic intellectual discipline, but rather just a special subject matter with its special jargon. If the "core" or "distribution" requirements produced little that was coherent in breadth, the narrow specialized major did not provide compensating coherence in depth. Nor did the faculties employ or promote the most powerful teaching devices or provide the best atmosphere for learning. They worked, over and over again, with about 10 percent of the student's mind: the part that memorizes facts and authoritative opinions and repeats them on exams for letter grades. Meanwhile, with little sense of community or common enterprise among students and faculty, the individual student, as a unique set of aptitudes and problems, was never engaged. One could go on, but perhaps this description of what must be the dominant experience of college among high school teachers helps to account for the almost universal criticism of the way our high school system prepares students for college.

The college curriculum can be a powerful recruiting device for teachers. A rich, intellectually satisfying curriculum will attract more complex, more adventurous, more powerful people to teaching. A thin, intellectually anemic, authoritarian college curriculum will attract those who will tolerate it. It will attract an anemic, passive prospective teacher, with predictable results for all of education for years to come. A recent report says that "a large majority of high school students say their class work is not very difficult, and almost two-thirds say that they would work harder if courses were more demanding or interesting." At the same time we know that many entering college are not ready for college work. Those in colleges who chronically bellyache about the poor preparation of their students might well ponder their own contribution to it.

SUCCESS AND ETHICS

We have not yet confronted the full consequences of the idea that one of the primary reasons for going to college is to be able to get a good job and make money. Sixty-nine percent of 2006 entering freshmen reported that "training for a specific career," "a better job," and "make more money" were very important reasons for their deciding to go to college. For a massive proportion of students and their parents, college as vocational training takes precedence over preparation for citizenship and even over personal development. As everyone knows, college graduates earn much more than high-school graduates. In the period 1992–96 the difference was 79.8 percent. According to some economists, the average student entering in 2003 would have a lifetime benefit from college of almost $300,000. Many a liberal arts college beset with financial problems has turned for survival to a curriculum designed to train students specifically for business, industry, and the professions; and for-profit colleges have sprung up on all sides for the same purpose.

It used to be thought that vocational aims were naturally inimical to the traditional aims of "liberal" education, and there is no question that narrowly vocational and professional curricula are not as conducive to the formation of the powers of independent judgment, to exercising the attributes of a free person, as is a curriculum of liberal studies. But the integration of study and work is now widely accepted in innovative curricula. Many colleges have found ways to reconcile business education in particular with studies in the liberal arts. Indiana University offers the Liberal Arts and Management Program. Claremont McKenna, Oberlin, Spelman, and dozens of other colleges have found promising ways to blend hitherto separated programs.

The bearing of the new curriculum on this idea is clear. Nothing prevents a strong, individual course of study from pointing to a lifetime of satisfying employment. Business leaders, we remember, report that "serious gaps now exist between the skills possessed by graduates and those required by today's high-performance jobs. The majority of students are severely lacking in flexible skills and attributes such as leadership, teamwork, problem solving, time management, adaptability, analytical thinking, global consciousness, and basic communications, including listening, speaking, reading and writing" (above, p. 3).

The need for these skills and attributes in *tomorrow*'s high-performance jobs is likely only to increase. For we have entered a period in which the whole world's economy is becoming more and more dependent on knowledge:

Knowledge is now recognised as being at least as important as capital (physical and financial) and natural resources as a source of economic growth. In short, knowledge is now regarded as an economic asset and the basis of national competitive advantage. . . .

. . . National policies for encouraging knowledge generation, knowledge acquisition, knowledge diffusion, and the exploitation of knowledge have become the most pressing priorities in the science, research, and education policy regimes. The emphasis, accordingly, has focused upon . . . the reform of knowledge institutions, together with a strong focus on so-called "human resources," or "human capital"; that is, people who know how to learn and who continue learning by upgrading existing skills and acquiring new skills. The knowledge economy is seen to demand meta-cognitive skills that are both broad and highly transferable, such as problem-solving and ability to learn.

In these terms, what we now offer the student seems inadequate, far from what the future will demand. The smorgasbord of courses, the random accumulation of credits, the lecture and exam system, the emphasis on memorization at the expense of other mental activities—seem designed to produce people who will be merely compliant, tolerably efficient subordinates, submissive to authority, and practiced in the passive consumption of predigested ideas. On the other hand, it should be clear that *there is a wonderful coincidence between the skills business leaders say they want for their top employees and future colleagues, and those that the new curriculum is designed to produce.*

But while we can applaud the capacity of our future graduates to "make it" in a newly competitive economic world, that is hardly all that we want for them or for us. It would be a cultural misfortune, and a subversion of the role of the college, if all we could produce were career training and economic success. Indeed, as Jim Sleeper has remarked, "There is a certain unresolved tension between the forces of global capitalism and the imperatives of a liberal-arts education and of liberal democracy itself." At Harvard, he continues,

> I held enough informal evening seminars and small discussions with students to see how bleak and burdened undergraduate life can be when competition is relentless and the bottom line is defined starkly in market terms.
>
> The danger now is that, under the guise of enhancing liberal-arts education for undergraduates—in universities feeling the pressure of corporate quarterly bottom lining here and abroad—a new kind of managerialism will train and seduce the most talented undergraduates into ways of knowing the world that render whole populations invisible and whole dimensions of ourselves inaccessible. . . .
>
> . . . when two thirds of some Ivy League senior class visit corporate recruiters, you can't help but wonder how many are banking their emotional and political prospects on technological and market promises of indefinite progress, promises that make the economically possible more important than the ethically permissible.

How do we ensure that our well-educated graduates will also be decent people and good citizens? Ever since I was a young graduate student, preparing to become a professor of literature in the wake of World War II, I have puzzled over the connection between scholarship and human decency. What good did the education and the vaunted scholarship of Germany do in the face of Nazism? We study values constantly, but how do we and our students come to practice them? The question is a difficult one, and there are reputable scholars who even consider it irrelevant. My friend and former colleague Stanley Fish has written recently that we are not "responsible for the effects of our teaching,"

> in fact, we are responsible only for its appropriate performance. That is, we are responsible for the selection of texts, the preparation of a syllabus, the sequence of assignments and exams, the framing and grading of a term paper, and so on.
>
> If, by the end of a semester, you have given your students an overview of the subject (as defined by the course's title and description in the catalog) and introduced them to the latest developments in the field and pointed them in the directions they might follow should they wish to inquire further, then you have done your job. What they subsequently do with what you have done is their business and not anything you should be either held to account for or praised for.

It may well be that neither can we control nor should we be held responsible for what kinds of people our students become; but we do in fact influence their values, whether we want to or not. We are in class and so are they.

On this premise, if on nothing more, most colleges hope to influence the character of their students, and many offer specific programs to this end. College catalogs are blooming these days with ethics requirements and ethics courses related to business, medical research, law, engineering, technology, sports, reproduction, and so on, and we know that the study of the humanities inherently raises all the great ethical issues. Whether formal courses produce virtuous behavior or just the study of virtue is anyone's guess, but higher education itself does some good. After an exhaustive survey, the respected researchers Ernest T. Pascarella and Patrick T. Terenzini conclude that the more education one has, the more likely one is to vote and to participate in various ways in the political process. Equally persuasive long-term evidence links education to more knowledgeable participation in a democratic society. "Overall, the evidence consistently indicates that college attendance has a positive effect on students' civic and community involvements . . . [and] a statistically significant, positive net effect on students' racial, ethnic, and multicultural attitudes and values" (2:336). The college years, then, do already make a difference.

Students' interactions with their peers have clear, statistically significant net effects on changes in various aspects of students' sociopolitical orientations, voting, social activism, liberalism, and support for civil liberties.

. . . volunteer community service has statistically significant, positive effects on civic and community-oriented or other-oriented attitudes and values. Participation in service-learning courses has even greater impact on students' commitment to community service, to helping others, to understanding community problems, and to volunteer work in the future. (2:339)

But apart from service-learning courses, the influence of the college curriculum seems disappointingly modest. Engineering curricula and study in math and other quantitative disciplines seem actually to inhibit students' social activism and progressive views on social issues. Otherwise, except in fields such as women's or ethnic studies, what students major in has little effect on their social or political values. "These findings suggest that *academic environments* [emphasis mine] may be more influential than a particular major field or discipline" (2:338).

I am certain that the "academic environment" accompanying the new curriculum has a meaningful effect on student values. In the first place, it promotes what Parker J. Palmer—in a remarkable essay—calls a new "dominant epistemology" or "mode of knowing":

My thesis is a very simple one: I do not believe that epistemology is a bloodless abstraction; the *way* we know has powerful implications for the *way* we live. I argue that every epistemology tends to become an ethic, and that every way of knowing tends to become a way of living. I argue that the relation established between the knower and the known, between the student and the subject, tends to become the relation of the living person to the world itself.

Palmer goes on to describe "objectivism," the dominant mode of knowing in what I have been calling the "old" curriculum. It has three familiar traits. In the first place, it is objective. It strenuously avoids subjectivity and personal bias. But in doing so, it creates a distance between what the scholar knows and his or her personal life. "It creates a world 'out there' of which we are only spectators and in which we do not live" (22). Next, it is analytic. Once something is objectified, it can be examined, cut up, and dissected—even killed. Finally, objectivism is "experimental": you can move the dissected pieces around, reshape them to please yourself, or just to see what happens.

Objectivism, the mode of knowing of most scholarly research, helps us create an accurate, realistic picture of the world, but at the same time it creates, by its very stance, a world that is fragmented and exploitable. It thus leads easily, in Palmer's terms, to "an ethic of competitive individualism." It must be held in creative tension with another, "relational," mode of knowing. Its intellectual distancing, its protection from subjectivity and bias, must not be allowed to destroy our capacity for "relatedness within individuals—relatedness not only to people but to events in history, to nature, to the world of ideas, and yes, to things of the spirit" (24).

To the extent that the new curriculum fosters this kind of relatedness, it will participate in a new epistemology and a new ethic. Palmer mentions studies—mostly interdisciplinary—that are not solely analytic and objective, but that at the same time compel engagement and involvement. We have seen that the pedagogy of the new curriculum, based squarely on involvement and community, runs strongly in this direction.

Another moral effect of the new curriculum will arise not from direct instruction but by example. A college that measures its success by the quality of student learning rather than by national prestige, a college that recruits good teachers rather than research stars—college professors who are obsessed with helping students rather than with their own publication records—creates an academic environment that is itself a powerful model of service to others.

The rhetoric of the new curriculum, too, is bound to be more exemplary than that of the old. In college today there is the advertised curriculum and the "hidden" one:

The professors' rhetoric may call for critical examination of diverse ideas, for creating one's own analyses and syntheses, for originality and developing one's own perspectives. But often, wittingly or unwittingly, evaluation and grading emphasize getting the right words in rote order or simple memorization for multiple-choice exams. Students quickly spot the disparity. They deliver what gets the best grade.

Even if unintended, this sort of implicit dishonesty—and it is widespread in the whole higher education environment—promotes anxiety, distrust, cynicism, gamesmanship, apathy, and student duplicity. It is true that a curriculum based on the confrontation of important issues can exert its own hidden pressures on the instructor's objectivity. But with its new commitment to honest dialogue as the central activity of learning, the new curriculum is overtly challenged to fulfill its own claims in a way that the old curriculum is not. It can thus provide an example of rhetorical integrity that deeply affects student values.

A pedagogy that is true to its own pronouncements, that lives on collective inquiry, that places students in the very condition of free citizens and engages them with the real-life consequences of ideas, promises to produce good scholarship and good people—and that is just what American democracy needs in this new century.

THE PACE OF CHANGE

The logic of the new curriculum is so persuasive, and constructive criticism of our present college system in recent years has been so consistent, that it is hard to doubt that American college education is indeed headed for change. The only question is, how soon will change begin to happen on a large scale? Looking at the obstacles, it is anyone's guess.

I will pass over the seemingly irreducible quota of anti-intellectualism in our national culture that expresses itself as hostility to colleges generally, except to note that much of our college culture is itself heavily unintellectual. We have observed that many students (like their parents) are primarily interested in college fun and sports, or at best in the diploma as a means to financial success. They are often openly contemptuous of study and faculty alike and care only about good grades, to which they take a consumerist attitude: "I paid my tuition; you can't give me Ds and Fs." They are major customers of term-paper dealers and other implements for doing as little work as possible. Colleges have been accused of "dumbing down" to satisfy these customers. By the very inertia of their stance, colleges are implicit opponents to change.

But there is some hope that students' hostility toward the curriculum is in part an implicit criticism of its failure to engage them, and that a more challenging curriculum would change some of their minds. Furthermore, there is a growing public realization that the typical faculty's conviction that "college as we teach it is good for you" is simply untrue for very many students. In a brilliant article that is worth citing at length, the high-school principal Rona Wilensky reports:

> I know bright students for whom academic questions
> hold no compelling interest. I know others who are not
> adept or well prepared for school subjects. Others have
> learning disabilities that make the academic tasks of
> schools both daunting and debilitating.
>
> I also know many students who have not had the privi-

lege of life circumstances that allow them to be successful in school. Some have been targets of systematic social oppression, some victims of family dysfunction; others have simply experienced long strings of bad luck.

Nevertheless, almost all my students have talents for and strong commitments to nonacademic pursuits. They are interested, talented, and often skilled in art, business, politics, sports, mechanics, music, and the myriad other activities that human beings engage in across our society. The trouble is that

almost all of them say they want to go to college. Why? Not because they love school and all things academic, but because American society has organized the transition from adolescence to adulthood in a way that makes college appear both necessary and inevitable . . . as the rubber stamp essential for access to jobs that pay well.

"College" as it is currently defined, she argues, is not only ill designed for the needs of these students but failing its own academic goals. She cites the 47 percent college graduation rate of students entering from high school, and the fact that in the 2003 National Survey of America's College Students "only 31 percent were proficient in the literacy tasks presented them."

Her conclusion, less pessimistic than one might at first expect, is not that we should give up on these students but that, among other things, we must change the design of "college" itself:

Let's step out of the existing paradigm of college preparation and its embedded assumption that academic skills, defined by academic prodigies, reflect some Platonic ideal of public education. Instead the focus should be on the skills, knowledge, and dispositions that all our citizens should possess. If we identify that list independently of college-entrance requirements and college professors' wish lists, it could focus on the real demands placed on citizens in a democracy and the real demands made by jobs that pay a living wage.

Significantly, we already know the broad outline of this list: substantive literacy, mathematical problem-solving, critical thinking, cross-cultural competency and related interpersonal skills, and the personal habits and dispositions to do high-quality work.

Wilensky envisions the rethinking of the whole enterprise of public schooling, including "a whole portfolio of postsecondary options that truly respond to both individual interests and strengths and society's various needs." As long as we have leaders in secondary education who think this way, there is room for hope.

But perhaps more effectively hostile than recalcitrant students are those trustees, officers, and staffs of colleges and universities, those program officers and trustees of educational foundations, and those officers of higher education associations whose business it is ostensibly to promote college education but who do so from the stance of the power they represent or serve. Typically, college presidents think of educational improvement in terms of money and of research prestige, of their college's going up in the national rankings, however blatantly irrelevant those rankings are. They confidently announce the goal of "making the top ten" (or the top hundred!), or trumpet the receipt of a multimillion-dollar alumni contribution that will be used to fund new endowed chairs for "faculty stars." Never mind that faculty stars with endowed chairs do not do much undergraduate teaching.

The massive influence on educational boards—if not complete control of them—by persons of wealth and political influence in the United States means that the ethics and attitudes of business and politics dominate the administration of our colleges. All these persons give lip service to "college education," but many of them have a very restricted notion of what that might mean. At bottom, this is nothing less than a conflict between cultures. As Roger W. Bowen puts it,

> The academic and political cultures are as far apart as they can be in the values they hold dear, the behavior they

accept, and the freedom they allow. . . . Some trustees take office with the missionary impulse to remake academe in the image of the corporation; others are intent on changing academic values to reflect the politics of the elected officials who appointed them to the board. Both groups may be hostile toward many of academe's traditions, including academic freedom, tenure, tolerance of unconventionality, and intellectual experimentation.

We may well wonder, then, how many boards or officers of our current institutions will sponsor more truly new campuses, truly new departures in higher education.

I have sufficiently described the problems with the faculties themselves. Anyone who knows them knows that they are composed largely of admirable and good people. But as I have tried to show, a great many of them have been trained and recruited for what has become the wrong curriculum, with which, however, they are mightily satisfied. Many of them simply do not belong in the college of the future, and it is not in their interest to promote changes to which they would be unlikely to adapt.

Despite the obstacles, we must remember that all the constituencies of college education contain persons of vision and fairness. Derek Bok, former president of Harvard, is perhaps our most profound critic of higher education, and in *Our Underachieving Colleges* he finds "the prospects for turning colleges into effective learning organizations . . . [n]ot good." Yet he still envisions the possibility of support from enlightened funding agencies and foundations, from boards of trustees, and from presidents and other academic leaders.

State governments, Bok points out, are "making the most visible efforts to induce colleges to improve," so far to small effect because of the crudeness of the measures and rewards they propose. "If state agencies and accreditors began to concentrate on each institution's processes for self-scrutiny and reform, college officials and their faculties would have to pay more attention to developing the procedures most likely to bring about educational progress" (331–32). Boards of trustees, he suggests, could

APPENDIX
Evergreen State College Sample Course Descriptions

The following descriptions are taken from Evergreen State College documents.

SCIENCE OF MIND

The Science of Mind Program will examine the scope and limits of recent attempts to develop a new science of cognition. It will explore these broad questions: What is involved in studying the mind scientifically? What questions can be answered scientifically? What questions can't? Is the mind nothing but the brain?

The program will contain the following interwoven threads:

COGNITIVE PSYCHOLOGY: . . . a variety of questions in the area of attention, memory, automatic processing, reasoning, and language as well as consciousness.

NEUROSCIENCE: . . . basic neurobiology (anatomy and physiology) with an emphasis on techniques used to obtain scientific understanding of neurophysiological processes.

STATISTICS/DATA ANALYSIS . . . will combine research design methods in psychology with an examination of the concepts and techniques of descriptive and inferential statistics, including multivariate statistics.

SEMINAR and related lectures will integrate the various elements of the program. . . .

PROJECTS: Each quarter there will be a group project. . . . In the Spring quarter, the bulk of the program work will consist in an extensive, original project. It will typically involve collaboration in developing a research problem, generating a research design, getting human subjects review approval, carrying out data collection, conducting data analysis, and presenting results. The aim is to actually conduct experimental cognitive scientific research. . . .

THE PHYSICIST'S WORLD

The twentieth century has brought about a revolution in our understanding of the physical universe. We have been forced to revise the way we think about even such basic concepts as space and time and causality, and about the properties of matter. An important part of this revolution has been the surprising discovery of fundamental ways in which our knowledge of the material world is ultimately limited. These limitations are not the result of surmountable shortcomings in human understanding, but are more deeply rooted in the nature of the universe itself.

In this program, we will examine the mental world created by the physicist so that we can make sense out of our experience of the material world, and try to understand the nature of physical reality. We will ask and explore answers to the twin questions of epistemology: What can we know? How can we know it? Starting with the Presocratic philosophers, we will continue through each major development of 20th-century physics, including the theories of relativity, quantum theory, deterministic chaos, and modern cosmology. We will examine the nature and the origins of the limits that each theory imposes on our ultimate knowledge of the world. We will read primary texts, such as works by the Presocratics, Plato, Lucretius, Galileo, Newton, and Einstein, as well as selected contemporary writings on physics. In addition to the other texts, a book-length manuscript has been written for this program that will serve as an extended outline and guide to the works and ideas we will read and discuss. Fall quarter will concentrate on the period up to the beginning of the 20th century; winter quarter will cover developments during the 20th century.

No mathematical prerequisites are assumed. Mathematical thinking will be developed within the context of the other ideas as needed for our purposes. The only prerequisites are curiosity about the natural world and a willingness to read and think and write about challenging texts and ideas. (Credit awarded in philosophy of science, history of science, introduction to physical science, introduction to mathematics and quantitative reasoning, and expository writing.)

BELIEF AND TRUTH

What do you believe and why? Can you prove it? How, or why not? Does it matter whether you can support what you believe? Is everything relative? Is science just another belief system? What are the roles of conjecture, evidence and theory in understanding? How can you articulate beliefs? How can you test hypotheses? What is the difference, if any? If these questions intrigue you, too, join us. Classes will include discussions, lectures, and other activities. Workshops may include quantitative reasoning, science, and statistical reasoning. Some online work may be required. (Credit awarded in sociology, history, statistics, philosophy of science, and/or conceptual physics.)

PUBLIC WORKS: DEMOCRACY AND DESIGN

The term "public works" refers to large-scale physical projects such as roads, waterworks, harbors or refuse-handling sites. Every community needs them. Indeed, most communities could not survive without these essential projects that allow us to live together as a civil collective. How long would civil society last if the garbage weren't being picked up, if clean water were not available, and if no transportation options were available? Yet, most communities struggle over their public works, and the outcomes are very often politically divisive and environmentally destructive. As such, the term "public works" can also refer to what it takes to make our public commons work.

We are interested in how to make our public projects work for us all, environmentally, ecologically and democratically. Our central question will be: In the present-day United States, how can public projects be designed ecologically and planned/implemented democratically?

The program faculty believe that the path to good answers goes through intelligent politics/administration and imaginative planning/engineering. In other words, good answers come out of good democracy and good design. This program will develop background in what it takes to achieve good democracy and good design, specifically in the nature and practice of American local politics and administration, and the theory and practice of ecologically sound civil engineering and planning. We do not require any specific background, although students will find it helpful to have solid experience and skill in at least one of the following: expository writing, community studies, graphic communication or ecological design.

Fall quarter will be organized around lectures and workshops on politics, administration, planning and engineering topics, case studies, and seminars on American society and culture, environmental affairs and human values. We will also lay the groundwork for winter quarter involvement in real-world public works projects in nearby communities. These projects will be a major component of winter quarter, alongside continued background development in democracy and design and seminars. (Credit awarded in writing, quantitative reasoning, political science, public and nonprofit administration, public works administration, community studies, civil engineering, environmental planning and design, and public policy.)

ASIAN CULTURE AND ART

This yearlong program will explore the expressive arts and cultures of four major Asian cultural regions: China, Japan, India and Indonesia. Our studies will include regional histories, philosophies and languages, and the theory and practice of Asian dance, music, theater, film, literature and other art forms. The ultimate goals of the program include an enhanced understanding of Asian expressive cultural traditions and the creation of performance pieces in the latter part of the year.

Weekly meetings will include lectures, hands-on workshops in the arts, presentations by visiting artists, films and seminars. Faculty members will offer lectures and workshops about each of the major cultural regions based on first-hand knowledge and experience, and the program will be supplemented with guest lectures and demonstrations.

Four workshops will be offered in the following Asian artistic traditions: Chinese opera, an ancient traditional Chinese theatrical performance style combining dance, music and theater; Japanese films and animation, their aesthetic, themes and techniques; Orissi dance, a 2,000-year-old classical dance tradition from eastern India; and Indonesian gamelan, a musical ensemble comprising bronze gongs, drums and metal xylophones.

Although each student will concentrate on one workshop, all students in the program will study all four cultural regions. Students will gain some experience in the major languages of each area (Mandarin, Japanese, Hindi/Oriya and Bahasa Indonesia). In general, the language instruction will place more emphasis on practical conversation in each culture.

Fall quarter will begin with an introduction to the four major cultural regions and will include both intensive reading and skill-building. In winter quarter, students will continue laying foundations in artistic skills while exploring some of the most important cultural concepts that underlie Asian expressive culture. Students will give a small program performance at the end of winter quarter to demonstrate their artistic skills and cultural understanding. The final work in the spring will vary by the chosen study. Students will spend the first two quarters gaining knowledge and skills to undertake self-initiated research projects that focus on any one or more of the studied cultures. These research projects will be the primary focus of the spring quarter for students who are not studying abroad.

The program will include two possibilities for study abroad.

Those studying Orissi dance will have the opportunity to travel to Orissa (India) during winter quarter to understand the process of postcolonial reconstruction of the oral art form from the sculptures on temple walls, the palm leaf manuscripts in the museums, and the living tradition in the villages of Orissa. They will also study under the foremost masters themselves. Students will return with skills to write an ethnographic research paper and do presentations of their understanding of the recreation of Orissi dance.

Students who do not travel will continue their studies on the Olympia campus during winter quarter. In spring, students interested in China may travel to China. They will visit the major cities and cultural sites, as well as learn about the arts and performance of ethnic minority groups. Students who are a good match for this program bring an open mind, a willingness to explore aspects of the world beyond the parameters of their current understanding, and the ability to recognize the wisdom in using body, mind and spirit in combination to deepen their knowledge of expressive culture. (Credit awarded in Asian studies, Asian languages [Mandarin, Japanese, Hindi/Oriya and Bahasa Indonesia], Asian arts, Asian expressive culture, performing and media arts and expository writing.)

SOURCE NOTES

Unless otherwise indicated, all my statistics come from the *Chronicle of Higher Education* 54.1 (2007), *Almanac* 2007–8 issue. Second references are by short title; the first reference may be found by using the index, under the author's name.

ABBREVIATIONS

AAC&U   The American Association of Colleges and Universities
CHE   *The Chronicle of Higher Education*
IHE   *Inside Higher Education,* newsroom@news.insidehighered
           .com

PREFACE

ix   University of California, Academic Senate, *Education at Berkeley,* Report of the Select Committee on Education (Berkeley, 1966).

x   Critiques of American higher education: For instance, Ernest L. Boyer, *Reinventing Undergraduate Education: A Blueprint for America's Research Universities* (Stony Brook: The Boyer Commission on Educating Undergraduates in the Research University, 1998); John Tagg, *The Learning Paradigm College* (Bolton, MA: Anker Publishing, 2003); David L. Kirp, *Shakespeare, Einstein, and the Bottom Line: The Marketing of Higher Education* (Cambridge, MA: Harvard UP, 2003); Derek Bok, *Universities in the Marketplace: The Commercialization of Higher Education* (Princeton: Princeton UP, 2003); Frank Newman, Lara Coutourier, and Jamie Scurry, *The Future of Higher Education: Rhetoric, Reality and the Risks of the Market* (San Francisco: Jossey-Bass, 2004); James Engell and Anthony Dangerfield, *Saving Higher Education in the Age of Money* (Charlottesville: U of Virginia P, 2005); Richard H. Hersh and John Merrow, eds., *Declining by Degrees: Higher Education at Risk* (New York: Palgrave Macmillan,

2005); Derek Bok, *Our Underachieving Colleges: A Candid Look at How Much Students Learn and Why They Should Be Learning More* (Princeton: Princeton UP, 2006); Harry R. Lewis, *Excellence without a Soul: How a Great University Forgot Education* (New York: Public-Affairs, 2006).

1 WHAT'S WRONG WITH COLLEGE

1   Poll by the *Chronicle:* "What Americans Think about Higher Education," May 2, 2003, A10–A16. See also Neil Gross and Solon Simmons, "Americans' Views of Political Bias in the Academy and Academic Freedom," AAUP working paper, May 22, 2006, http://www.aaup.org/surveys/2006Gross.pdf, esp. pp. 4–7.

1   Students think they're doing fine: AAC&U, *Liberal Education Outcomes: A Preliminary Report on Student Achievement in College* (Washington, DC: AAC&U, 2005), part 4.

2   Proficiency statistics: AAC&U, *Liberal Education Outcomes,* part 5. The 2003 report "National Assessment of Adult Literacy," issued by the National Center for Education Statistics, rates only about 30 percent of adults having college degrees as "proficient" in reading—that is, as capable of "using printed and written information to function in society, to achieve one's goals, and to develop one's knowledge and potential" (2, 38); http://nces.ed.gov/Pubs2007/2007480.pdf.

3   "spokesman for the National Alliance for Business": Milton Grossberg in *Crosstalk* (National Center for Public Policy and Higher Education) 8.2 (Spring 2000): 12–13.

3   Colleges as commercial establishments: See Henry A. Giroux, "Selling Out Higher Education," *Policy Futures in Education* 1.1 (2003): 179–200 (online journal available at http://www.wwwords.co.uk/pfie); Donald G. Stein, ed., *Buying In or Selling Out? The Commercialization of the American Research University* (New Brunswick, NJ: Rutgers UP, 2004).

4   Engell and Dangerfield, *Saving Higher Education,* 2.

5   Department of Education study: Elizabeth A. Jones et al., *National Assessment of College Student Learning: Identifying College Graduates' Essential Skills in Writing, Speech and Listening, and Critical Thinking,* Final Project Report, National Center for Education Statistics (Washington, DC: U.S. Department of Education, Office of Educational Research and Improvement, 1995), 167, 165.

7   On the increasing use of adjunct or part-time faculty, see the reports and surveys of the Coalition on the Academic Work Force: http:www.academicworkforce.org/data.

8   Teachers as exploited labor: On academic labor conditions, see Marc Bousquet, *How the University Works: Higher Education and the Low Wage Nation* (New York: New York UP, 2008).

8   Rebekah Nathan (pseud.), *My Freshman Year: What a Professor Learned by Becoming a Student* (Ithaca: Cornell UP, 2006); quotation from a review by Diana Jean Schemo, *New York Times,* 23 August 2006.

10   Professional and liberal education: See the report of the National Leadership Council for Liberal Education and America's Promise, *College Learning for the New Global Century* (Washington, DC: AAC&U, 2007).

10   "new design for higher education": Perhaps the best brief summary of new thinking is AAC&U's *College Learning for the New Global Century.*

2   AN ENVIRONMENT FOR LEARNING

11   My opening discussion of teaching is heavily indebted to Donald L. Finkel, *Teaching with Your Mouth Shut* (Portsmouth, NH: Boynton/ Cook, 2000), 5–8.

12   T. Kaori Kitao, "The Usefulness of Uselessness," keynote address, 1999 Institute for the Academic Advancement of Youth's Odyssey, Swarthmore College, March 27, 1999.

12   Marshall Spector, "'Look at Me': A Teaching Primer," *CHE,* September 27, 2002, B15.

13   Ken Bain, *What the Best College Teachers Do* (Cambridge, MA: Harvard UP, 2004), 108–9. Bain does not exclude the large lecture, in the right hands, from possibly providing the desired student experience.

17   Engineering education: Domenico Grasso, "Is it Time to Shut Down Engineering Colleges?" *IHE,* September 23, 2005; Committee on the Engineer of 2020, *The Engineer of 2020: Visions of Engineering in the New Century* (Washington, DC: National Academy of Engineering, 2005); Rosalind Williams, "Education for the Profession Formerly Known as Engineering," *CHE,* January 24, 2003, B13. In *Retooling: A Historian Confronts Technological Change* (Cambridge, MA: MIT P, 2002), Williams writes: "The convergence of technological and liberal arts education is a deep, long-term, and irreversible trend. . . . Students need to be educated in an environment where they get used to justifying and explaining their approach to solving problems and also to dealing with people who have other ways of defining and solving problems. Only a hybrid educational environment will prepare engineering students for

handling technoscientific life in a hybrid world" (82–83). See also James J. Duderstadt, *Engineering for a Changing World* (Ann Arbor: Millennium Project, U of Michigan, 2008), esp. 48–56.

17   Science education: James M. Bower, "Scientists and Science Education Reform: Myths, Methods, and Madness," www.nas.edu/rise/backg2a.htm; Erik Stokstad, "Reintroducing the Intro Course," *Science* 293 (August 2001): 1608–10; Emory University, Center for Science Education, "Problem-based Learning Links," *Science Net,* http://www.cse.emory.edu/sciencenet/coll_curr/pbl_links.html; *Bio 2010: Transforming Undergraduate Education for Future Research Biologists* (Washington, DC: National Research Council of the National Academies, 2003); "Science and Engaged Learning," *Peer Review* 7.2 (2005).

18   Howard Hughes Medical Institute: *IHE,* March 23, 2005.

18   Strawberry Creek College: The following account has previously appeared, with slight differences, in the *Chronicle of the University of California* 5 (2002): 103–14.

19   Joseph Tussman, *The Beleaguered College: Essays on Educational Reform* (Berkeley: Institute of Governmental Studies P, U of California, 1997), chaps. 1 and 2. The experimental college idea of designing full-time "programs" instead of individual courses for students was crucially influential in the later design of Evergreen State College. See Barbara Leigh Smith et al., *Learning Communities: Reforming Undergraduate Education* (San Francisco: Jossey-Bass, 2004), 36–43.

25   Jonathan Harris, "Overview of the Programs and General Philosophy," Collegiate Seminar Program, June 1979, 5.

26   Alexander W. Astin, *Achieving Educational Excellence* (San Francisco: Jossey-Bass, 1985), 33.

27   Mandelbaum Committee, "A Report on the Collegiate Seminar Program (Strawberry Creek College)," received by the Chancellor's Office December 12, 1975.

28   Program sponsors an individual major: Collegiate Seminar Program "Program Plan for 1977–78," 3–4.

30   Program leaders' statement: "The Collegiate Seminar Program: A Summary Description," submitted to the Committee on Educational Policy, spring 1979.

30   Ad Hoc Committee on the Collegiate Seminar Program, report to Associate Vice Chancellor Riley, June 14, 1979, ii.

32   Ad Hoc Committee on the Collegiate Seminar Program, letter to the Committee on Educational Policy, November 16, 1979.

32   Committee on Educational Policy, letter to Associate Vice-Chancellor Riley, November 12, 1979, 3.

34   Committee on Academic Planning, "Notice of Meeting," Berkeley Division of the Academic Senate, May 20, 1974, 10.

3   FACULTY RESPONSIBILITY TO STUDENTS

36   Faculty reports: See, e.g., Harvard University, Faculty of Arts and Sciences, "Harvard College Curricular Review," Report of the Committee on General Education, November 2005, http.www.fas.harvard.edu/curriculum-review/gen ed report 05.pdf; Yale University, "Report on Yale College Education," April 2003, http:// www.yale.edu/yce/report/cycereport.pdf, and http://www.yale.edu/yalecollege/freshmen/special/seminars; University of Pennsylvania, School of Arts and Sciences, Curriculum Review Initiative, http://www.sas.upenn.edu/faculty/Curriculum_Review/.

36   Educational associations and foundations: A compendious account of major problems with the curriculum will be found in *Integrity in the College Curriculum: A Report to the Academic Community,* The Findings and Recommendations of the Project on Redefining the Meaning and Purpose of Baccalaureate Degrees (Washington, DC: Association of American Colleges, 1985; 2nd ed. 1990). The AAC&U, the Pew Charitable Trusts, the John S. and James L. Knight Foundation, and the Carnegie Foundation for the Advancement of Teaching, beginning with the work of its former head Ernest Boyer, have led thinking on this subject.

36   In the ensuing paragraphs I borrow ideas from my "Faculty Responsibility for the Curriculum," *Academe* 71 (1985): 18–21, which I think is still, unfortunately, much to the point.

37   Departments and majors: See also Richard Edwards, "The Academic Department: How Does It Fit into the University Reform Agenda?," *Change* 31.5 (September–October 1999): 17–27.

38   National Education Goals: Panel [1990], Goal 6 (Adult Literacy and Lifelong Learning), http://www.negp.gov/page3-13.htm; and Jones et al., *National Assessment of College Student Learning,* esp. 165–67.

38   Generic skills: Sam Wineburg, "Teaching the Mind Good Habits," *CHE,* April 11, 2003, B20, makes the case that scholars from different disciplines read, and therefore think, in significantly different ways. However, I cannot follow him to the extreme conclusion "that there is no such thing as generic critical thinking."

39   Academic disciplines: For a detailed definition, see Arthur King

and John Brownell, *The Curriculum and the Disciplines of Knowledge* (New York: Wiley, 1966), 67–98.

40 Definition of a major: From a report by the National Commission for Excellence in Teacher Education, quoted in *CHE*, March 6, 1985.

41 Breadth and depth: A notable attempt to describe college curricula, based on a representative sample of thirty colleges, is reported by Robert Zemsky in *Structure and Coherence: Measuring the Undergraduate Curriculum* (Washington, DC: Association of American Colleges, 1989). Zemsky and his colleagues adopt a conventional notion of breadth ("experience . . . in humanities, social science, and natural sciences including mathematics" [16]). Their conception of depth is somewhat more interesting ("Is there a sequence of courses—that is—, a path through the curriculum that requires a student to use the knowledge and techniques gained in introductory courses in intermediate and advanced courses?" [19]). In this scheme, the sciences as currently taught have the most "depth" and the humanities the least (20–21).

4 A CURRICULUM DESIGN FOR THE FUTURE

43 Student learning: The following is an informal summary of, among other sources, Arthur W. Chickering and Zelda Gamson, "Seven Principles for Good Practice in Undergraduate Education," *AAHE Bulletin* 39.7 (1987): 3–7; Arthur W. Chickering and Linda Reisser, *Education and Identity,* 2nd ed. (San Francisco: Jossey-Bass, 1993), esp. 316–91; James L. Ratcliff, "Quality and Coherence in General Education," and Roberta S. Matthews et al., "Creating Learning Communities," in *Handbook of the Undergraduate Curriculum,* ed. Jerry G. Gaff et al. (San Francisco: Jossey-Bass, 1997), 141–69 and 457–75, respectively; George D. Kuh et al., *Student Success in College: Creating Conditions That Matter* (San Francisco: Jossey-Bass, 2005); David Guile, "From 'Credentialism' to the 'Practice of Learning': Reconceptualising Learning for the Knowledge Economy," *Policy Futures in Education* 1.1 (2003): 83–104.

44 The rationale for interdisciplinary courses has been excellently outlined by James R. Davis in *Interdisciplinary Courses and Team Teaching: New Arrangements for Learning* (Phoenix: American Council on Education/Oryx, 1995). While Davis bases his observations solely on courses involving "two or more professors collaborating in significant ways" (5), his general remarks apply equally well to courses taught by individual professors who make significant connections to areas outside their own disciplines. Davis outlines the

arguments for interdisciplinary study as a corrective to various defects in the disciplines, such as their isolation, absoluteness, reductionism, and trivialism (35–37); but in the present context, the leading argument for interdisciplinary study is its positive connection to learning. As Davis puts it:

> First, there is a growing belief that the goal of education today should no longer be dominated by the concern for transmitting information. . . . Having knowledge is different from having information, and gaining knowledge today involves multiple perspectives and complex processes that students learn best in classrooms where interdisciplinary courses are offered and traditional teaching is augmented by other strategies.
>
> Second, students today live in a world . . . where problems appear to pile up faster than solutions. . . . Unfortunately, none of these problems come in the tidy packages of disciplines. . . . Although the fundamental research created by the disciplines may be indispensable in addressing certain aspects of these problems, ultimate solutions require people who are skilled in using many kinds of knowledge in a problem-solving context. . . . Effective problem solvers today have skills in seeing the "big picture," in creating webs of interrelated knowledge, and in working in teams. Thus, interdisciplinary courses, it can be argued, are well-suited to developing the problem-solving skills most needed in today's society because they emphasize the development of comprehensive perspectives. (38–39)

See also Julie Thompson Klein, *Interdisciplinarity: History, Theory, and Practice* (Detroit: Wayne State UP, 1990), esp. 163–81.

45   "desired outcomes of undergraduate education": See AAC&U, National Panel Report, chap. 3, "The Learning All Students Need for the 21st Century," www.greaterexpectations.com; and *Liberal Education Outcomes: A Preliminary Report on Student Achievement in College* (Washington, DC: AAC&U, 2005).

45   Aalborg University: Quotation from http://en.aau.dk/About+Aalborg+University/Academic+Profile.

47   "bodily presence" in the classroom: Hubert L. Dreyfus, *On the Internet* (London: Routledge, 2001).

47   "'distance' from the instructor": Lee Herman and Alan Mandell, *From Teaching to Mentoring: Principle and Practice, Dialogue and Life in Adult Education* (London: Routledge and Falmer, 2004), 144–47, 182–83; their chap. 8 makes a persuasive case for the possibilities of

"dialogical community" in virtual reality. See also Kuh, *Student Success in College*, 282–83.

47 On the prevalence of online education, see the report by Elaine Allen and Jeff Seaman, *Making the Grade: Online Education in the United States, 2006* (Needham, MA: Sloan Consortium, 2006), http://www.sloan-c.org/publications/survey/pdf/making_the_grade.pdf.

48 Future economies of distance learning: Carol Twigg, "Improving Learning and Cutting Costs," *IHE*, November 2, 2005.

48 Growth of open sources: http://ocw.mit.edu; http://cnx.org; http://www.ocicu.org.

50 Class attendance at Berkeley: Figures are averages calculated from tables published by the University of California Undergraduate Experience Survey, http://osr.berkeley.edu/Public/surveys/ucues/2004/sp2004_counts.htm.

51 Student study time: Worse, the National Survey of Student Engagement Annual Report 2007, "Experiences That Matter: Enhancing Student Learning and Success," based on 300,000 students attending 587 colleges, puts the figure at 13–14 hours per week, http://nsse.iub.edu/NSSE%5F2007%5FAnnual%5FReport/.

51 Cheating: The large survey by the Duke Center for Academic Integrity also reports: "In most campuses, 70% of students admit to some cheating. Close to one-quarter of the participating students admitted to serious test cheating in the past year and half admitted to one or more instances of serious cheating on written assignments." See http://www.academicintegrity.org/cai_research.asp.

51 Grade inflation: See, e.g., John Merrow, "Grade Inflation: It's Not Just an Issue for the Ivy League," *Carnegie Perspectives,* June 2004, http://www.carnegiefoundation.org/perspectives/perspectives 2004.June.html.

51 Graduation rates: *CHE,* August 26, 2005, 14.

51 Carnegie Foundation report: Anne Colby et al., *Educating Citizens: Preparing America's Undergraduates for Lives of Civic and Moral Responsibility* (San Francisco: Jossey-Bass, 2003), 132–33.

55 Assessment and the public: See the report of the National Commission on Accountability in Higher Education, *Accountability for Better Results: A National Imperative for Higher Education* (Denver: State Higher Education Executive Officers, 2005), http://www.sheeo.org/account/accountability.pdf; and John V. Lombardi, "Accountability, Improvement and Money," *IHE,* May 3, 2005.

55 Literature on assessment: See, e.g., Gaff, *Handbook of the Undergraduate Curriculum,* 571–607 and refs.; Addison Greenwood, *National*

Assessment of College Student Learning: Getting Started, National Center for Education Statistics (Washington, DC, 1993); Trudy W. Banta et al., *Making a Difference: Outcomes of a Decade of Assessment in Higher Education* (San Francisco: Jossey-Bass, 1993); Jones et al., *National Assessment of College Student Learning;* Trudy W. Banta et al., eds., *Building a Scholarship of Assessment* (San Francisco: Jossey-Bass, 2002). A comprehensive account of problems and possibilities is contained in the series of three reports issued by the Educational Testing Service under the rubric *A Culture of Evidence* (Princeton: Educational Testing Service, 2006–8). The Department of Education has recently made a major grant to a group of three academic associations led by the AAC&U to assess existing tools and develop new ones for measuring student skills.

55 National Survey of Student Engagement: http://nsse.iub.edu/index.cfm.

55 Collegiate Learning Assessment Project: http://www.cae.org/content /pro_collegiate.htm; Richard H. Hersh, "What Does College Teach?," *Atlantic Monthly,* November 2005; *CHE,* June 6, 2008, A1, A18.

56 College rankings: Amy Graham and Nicholas Thompson, "Breaking Ranks," *Washington Monthly,* September 2001.

56 Public institutions: Some successful assessments are reported in the article "Does 'Value Added' Add Value?," *IHE,* November 3, 2006.

57 1998 survey: Marvin W. Peterson and Derek S. Vaughan, "Promoting Academic Improvement," in Banta, *Building a Scholarship of Assessment,* 31–33.

58 Alverno: Alverno College Faculty, *Student Assessment-as-Learning at Alverno College* (Milwaukee: Alverno College Institute, 1994), 4. In the present discussion I rely on the compact account in *Student Assessment-as-Learning* (from which I quote further below); on the more detailed account of the Alverno philosophy of education in Marcia Mentkowski et al., *Learning That Lasts: Integrating Learning, Development, and Performance in College and Beyond* (San Francisco: Jossey-Bass, 2000); and on a visit to the college.

61 "recent study of other successful efforts": Mentkowski, *Learning That Lasts,* appendix H; Carl J. Waluconis, "Student Self-Evaluation," in Banta, *Making a Difference,* 244–55.

61 Assessment design: Trudy W. Banta, "Characteristics of Effective Outcomes Assessment," in Banta, *Building a Scholarship of Assessment,* 262–79, lists these and additional desirable characteristics.

61 Student questionnaires: A recent study of 50,000 enrollments by

three economists at Ohio State finds strong student biases and only a weak relationship between student learning and student evaluations of faculty. See Bruce A. Weinberg et al., "Evaluating Methods for Evaluating Instruction: The Case of Higher Education," National Bureau of Economic Research, working paper no. 12844 (2007), http://www.nber.org/papers/w12844.

61 1998 survey: Peterson and Vaughan, "Promoting Academic Improvement," 36.

62 Peer review: See also Pat Hutchings, "The Peer Collaboration and Review of Teaching," in *The Professional Evaluation of Teaching,* by James England, Pat Hutchings, and Wilbert J. McKeachie, ACLS occasional paper no. 33 (New York: ACLS, 1996), 9–17.

62 "traditional methods of evaluating teachers": Described in "Results of the National Survey on the Reexamination of Faculty Roles and Rewards, 1994," in *Scholarship Assessed: Evaluation of the Professoriate,* by Charles E. Glassick, Mary Taylor Huber, and Gene I. Maeroff (San Francisco: Jossey Bass, 1997), appendix B, tables 18–27.

5   TOWARD A NEW CURRICULUM

63 Robert B. Barr and John Tagg, "From Teaching to Learning: A New Paradigm for Undergraduate Education," *Change,* November/December 1995, 13–25, http://critical.tamucc.edu/~blalock/readings/tch2learn.htm; and Tagg, *The Learning Paradigm College.*

63 Alexander W. Astin, "How Liberal Arts Colleges Affect Students," *Daedalus* 128.1 (1999): 77.

64 Harvard faculty vote on General Education Curriculum, May 15, 2007: http://www.fas.harvard.edu/~secfas/Harvard_FAS_Vote_Establishing_New_Program_in_General_Education.pdf.

65 Criteria for Harvard courses in the eight areas (qtd. from Harvard faculty vote): Under Aesthetic and Interpretive Understanding, courses should not only "develop skills in criticism" but also "include experiences outside the classroom, such as visits to exhibitions . . . or allow students to undertake creative work."

Under Culture and Belief, qualifying courses must "draw connections between material covered in the course and cultural issues of concern or interest that are likely to arise in students' own lives."

Courses in Empirical and Mathematical Reasoning must not only "teach the conceptual and theoretical tools used in reasoning and problem-solving, such as statistics, probability, mathematics, logic, and decision theory" but also "apply these tools to problems of wide concern."

Ethical Reasoning courses must entail "competing conceptions and theories of ethical concepts such as the good life, obligation, rights, justice, and liberty," and their application to "concrete ethical dilemmas" of the sort students will encounter "in medicine, law business, politics, and daily life."

Courses in both Science of Living Systems and Science of the Physical Universe not only "introduce key concepts, facts, and theories" relevant to the subject area but also relate them "to problems of wide concern."

Courses in both Societies of the World and The United States in the World must "relate the material studied to the kinds of social, cultural, political, legal, linguistic, or economic issues students might encounter in a global context."

In addition, the faculty specifies that qualifying courses "be taught, to the extent practicable, in interactive formats that give students an opportunity to discuss the material with the faculty member teaching the class and with one another."

66 Changes to core curricula: Alan F. Edwards Jr., *Interdisciplinary Undergraduate Programs: A Directory,* 2nd ed. (Acton, MA: Copley, 1996), 426–28.

67 John Sexton, "The Common Enterprise University and the Teaching Mission," November 2004, 5, http://www.nyu.edu/about/sexton-teachingmission04.html.

67 Civic engagement programs: See *IHE,* January 28, 2008.

67 George Mason: http://www.ncc.gmu.edu/programs/fye.

68 Arizona State: http://shesc.asu.edu.

68 Arizona State West: http://www.west.asu.edu/sbs/aboutSBS/degrees/iss.htm.

68 Clemson: http://www.clemson.edu/ugs/creative_inquiry.

69 Learning communities: Quotation from Smith, *Learning Communities,* 20; see also Matthews et al., "Creating Learning Communities," 458.

69 The National Learning Communities Project, directed by the Washington Center for Improving the Quality of Undergraduate Education at Evergreen State College and supported by the Pew Charitable Trusts, has contact with some hundreds of participating colleges and maintains a directory of learning community initiatives. Over 20 percent of the programs recently surveyed offer coordinated curricula, almost a third involve service- or community-based learning, a third offer residential arrangements, and some 15 percent are online or involve technical components. The

directory is available at http://www.evergreen.edu/washcenter/06_directory_search_s.asp.

69 Federated Learning Communities, Stony Brook: http://www.sunysb.edu/flcglobal/Spring2003/Syllabus.htm.

70 Holy Cross: http://www.holycross.edu/montserrat/learning.

70 Bailey Scholars Program: http://www.bsp.msu.edu.

71 Tufts: "Writing Across the Curriculum at Tufts University," http://ase.tufts.edu/wac/about.asp.

71 Honors programs: The National Collegiate Honors Council offers descriptions of the basic characteristics of honors programs and honors colleges at http://www.nchchonors.org/basic.htm, and http://www.nchchonors.org/HonorsBasicChars.

72 University of Virginia: http://artsandsciences.virginia.edu/college/imp/index.html.

72 King's College honors program: http://www.kings.edu/frames/tb_frames/academics.html.

72 Lee Honors College, Western Michigan: Course catalogs are available at www.wmich.edu/honors/coursecatalogs.html.

72 New College, University of Alabama: www.as.ua.edu/nc.

73 Howard Lowry, "Wooster: Adventure in Education," *College of Wooster Bulletin* 39, no. 7 (December 1945): 21.

74 Wooster faculty study leaves: College of Wooster, "Statute of Instructions," section 11.A.2.

74 Loren Pope, *Colleges That Change Lives,* rev. ed. (New York: Penguin Books, 2000), 245.

6   THE NEW CURRICULUM: SOME INNOVATIVE COLLEGES

75 Fairhaven College: The ensuing discussion is based on a personal visit and on two publications available from the college: "The Student Guide to Fairhaven College, 2004–05" and "Fairhaven College Fall 2004 Class Descriptions."

77 Gallatin: Discussion is based on a personal visit, and on *New York University Bulletin* 104.6 (April 5, 2004): 35–47, Gallatin School of Individualized Study.

78 St. John's College: http://www.stjohnscollege.edu/asp/home.aspx.

78 Other "great books" schools: Tiny Shimer College in Chicago bases its innovative curriculum, called Shared Inquiry, on a somewhat more multicultural list.

78 Colleges devoted to study of the environment: For lists of these colleges and of other ecological curricula, see http://www.naage.org/ and http://www.ecoleague.org/.

79   Bennington, original principles: Bennington College, "Symposium Report of the Bennington College Board of Trustees," June 1994.

81   Bennington guidelines: Bennington College, "The Bennington Plan," March 21, 2001.

82   Elizabeth Coleman, "The Arts and Society: Looking Ahead," from a speech presented at the Getty Center, February 1998, http://www.bennington.edu/education/faculty/recent_newswork/coleman.htm.

83   Steven J. Tepper, "The Creative Campus: Who's No. 1?," *CHE,* October 1, 2004, B6–B8.

83   Hampshire College: Account based on visits to the college, information on the college Web site, and on *Non Satis Non Scire,* the college policy handbook.

85   Empire State College: This account of mentoring at Empire State is based on the college Web site, http://www.esc.edu/esconline/online2.nsf/ESChome.html, partly on a restricted area to which I was kindly given access by Professor Alan Mandell, Director of the Mentoring Institute; and on Herman and Mandell, *From Teaching to Mentoring,* an account of the authors' mentoring philosophy, supported with numerous case studies from their practice at the college.

88   History of Evergreen State College: A brief account of the early history of the college is provided by Barbara Leigh Smith, "Evergreen at Twenty-Five: Sustaining Long-Term Innovation," in *Reinventing Ourselves: Interdisciplinary Education, Collaborative Learning, and Experimentation in Higher Education,* ed. Barbara Leigh Smith and John McCann (Bolton, MA: Anker, 2001), 65–90.

88   The following description of Evergreen is based on information from the college Web site (www.evergreen.edu) and from numerous college documents and publications gathered in the course of campus visits.

88   Expectations of a graduate: http://www.evergreen.edu/aboutevergreen/expectations.htm.

94   DEEP project: The major findings of the project are reported in Kuh, *Student Success in College.*

94   Final report: NSSE Institute for Effective Educational Practice, "Final Report: The Evergreen State College," October 31, 2003, http://www.evergreen.edu/provost/documents.htm, DEEP document.

95   Evergreen accreditation report: Ernest E. Ettlich, "Regular Interim Report: The Evergreen State College," for the Northwest Commis-

sion on Colleges and Universities, October 30–31, 2003, 11, http://
www.evergreen.edu/provost/docs/Evaluation%20Report.pdf.

7 RESEARCH, SCHOLARSHIP, TEACHING, AND THE EDUCATION OF PROFESSORS

99   Ernest L. Boyer, *Scholarship Reconsidered: Priorities of the Professoriate* (Princeton: Carnegie Foundation, 1990).

99   Colleges adopting Boyer's definitions: Western Carolina University, Northeastern State University, New Century College (George Mason University); see *IHE,* October 2, 2007.

106 "production of scholarly monographs": See the articles by the Harvard University Press editor Lindsay Waters: "Rescue Tenure from the Tyranny of the Monograph," *CHE,* April 20, 2001, B7–B10; and "A Call for Slow Writing," *IHE,* March 10, 2008. See also "Report of the MLA Task Force on Evaluating Scholarship for Tenure and Promotion (2006)," in *Profession 2007* (New York: MLA, 2007), esp. 29–41, http://www.mla.org/tenure_promotion. Incidentally, the task force reports that emphasis on the importance of publication for tenure and promotion has increased in the past ten years, and that the percentage (75.7%) of departments rating scholarship (i.e., publication) of primary importance (over teaching) has more than doubled since 1968 (10).

109 Jonathan Z. Smith, "The Necessary Lie: Duplicity in the Disciplines," in *Teaching at Chicago,* ed. Diane M. Emerson (Chicago: U of Chicago Center for Teaching and Learning, 1990), 3, http://teaching.uchicago.edu/handbook.tac.html.

109 Tufts: *Bulletin of Tufts University,* http://ase.tufts.edu/bulletin.

110 John Dewey, *Democracy and Education* (New York: Macmillan, 1916), 188.

113 Doctor of arts degree: See Judith S. Glazer, *A Teaching Doctorate? The Doctor of Arts Degree, Then and Now* (Washington, DC: American Association for Higher Education, 1993).

113 "misgivings about the Ph.D.": Prominent among these is the project Re-Envisioning the Ph.D, funded by the Pew Charitable Trusts and centered at the University of Washington. I am greatly indebted to the project for bibliographical materials and other assistance to the ensuing discussion. See also Association of American Universities Committee on Graduate Education, "Report and Recommendations," October 1998, http://aau.edu/reports/GradEdRpt.html. In 2002 the Carnegie Foundation established the Carnegie Initiative on the Doctorate, with 50 partner departments involv-

ing six fields of study; http://www.carnegiefoundation.org/CID. The project Preparing Future Faculty, long sponsored by the AAC&U and the Council of Graduate Schools, was unusually aware of the disparity between graduate preparation and the reality of teaching experience. See http://www.preparing-faculty.org/.

113 Statistics on attrition: Comprehensive statistics on doctoral education can be found in William G. Bowen and Neil L. Rudenstine et al., *In Pursuit of the Ph.D.* (Princeton: Princeton UP, 1992). See 124 ff. for completion rates; the median elapsed time to degree they report is almost seven years (114). The Council of Graduate Schools is currently conducting a long-term study, the Ph.D. Completion Project; preliminary figures are reported in *Ph.D. Completion and Attrition: Analysis of Baseline Program Data* (Washington, DC: CGS, 2007).

115 Badness of most dissertations: The scholarly publisher William Germano contributes a rare treatment of this topic in "If Dissertations Could Talk, What Would They Say?" *CHE*, June 13, 2003, B9–B10.

115 Mentoring of graduate students: Jody D. Nyquist and Bettina J. Woodford, *Re-envisioning the Ph.D.: What Concerns Do We Have?* (Seattle: Center for Instructional Development and Research, U of Washington, 2000), 20; http//www.grad.washington.edu/envision/project_resources/concerns.html.

116 Interdisciplinary graduate studies: The collaborative possibilities of graduate training are usefully stressed by David Damrosch in "Mentors and Tormentors in Doctoral Education," *CHE*, November 17, 2000, B24. See also *IHE*, April 15, 2005; *IHE*, May 17, 2006; and http//mba.yale.edu.

118 Institutes for research: See Murray Sperber, "How Undergraduate Education Became College Lite," in Hersh and Merrow, *Declining by Degrees,* 141–42.

8   FINAL PROBLEMS

120 "push toward ever greater selectivity": See Deirdre Henderson's spirited essay "Reforming Selective College Admissions," *IHE,* February 28, 2006.

120 "gap in college going": See Thomas J. Kane, "College-Going and Inequality," in *Social Inequality,* ed. Kathryn M. Neckerman (New York: Russell Sage, 2004), 320; Robert B. Reich, "How Selective Colleges Heighten Inequality," *CHE*, September 15, 2000.

120 "outreach and scholarship plans": Exemplary programs are the

University of Virginia's AccessUVa and College Guide Program; see *CHE,* April 22, 2005, B12.

120 "culture of higher learning": Smith, *Learning Communities,* 101-3, cites particularly in this regard the work of Kenneth Bruffee at Brooklyn College; see Bruffee, *Collaborative Learning: Higher Education, Interdependence, and the Authority of Knowledge* (Baltimore: Johns Hopkins UP, 1993).

121 "Future teachers": Below are summarized some views found in my "Prospective Teachers and the Liberal Arts Curriculum," *Journal of Thought* 17.4 (1982): 3-14.

121 The Education Trust, "Youth at the Crossroads," a report to the National Commission on the High School Senior Year, 2000, quoted by Tagg, *The Learning Paradigm College,* 43.

122 "A recent report": Michael Janofsky, "Students Say High Schools Let Them Down," *New York Times,* July 16, 2005, A8.

122 "not ready for college work": Tamar Lewin, "Many Going to College Aren't Ready, Report Finds," *New York Times,* August 17, 2005, A13.

123 Earnings of college graduates: See Ernest T. Pascarella and Patrick T. Terenzini, *How College Affects Students,* vol. 2: *A Third Decade of Research* (San Francisco: Jossey-Bass, 2005), 453; Lisa Barrow and Cecilia Elena Rouse, "Does College Still Pay?," *The Economist's Voice* 2.4 (2005): article 3.

123 Combining business and liberal education: See David Paris, *Business and the Liberal Arts: Integrating Professional and Liberal Education* (Washington, DC: The Council of Independent Colleges, 2007); http://www.indiana.edu/~lamp/; *IHE,* February 1, 2008.

124 World's economy dependent on knowledge: Michael A. Peters and Walter Humes, "Education in the Knowledge Economy," *Policy Futures in Education* 1.1 (2003): 1-2.

125 Jim Sleeper: "Harvard's New Leader, Global Capitalism, and the Liberal Arts," *CHE,* April 13, 2001, B20.

126 Stanley Fish: "Aim Low: Confusing Democratic Values with Academic Ones Can Easily Damage the Quality of Education," *CHE,* May 16, 2003, C5.

126 Ethics courses in college: See Bok, *Our Underachieving Colleges,* 150-71; Colby et al., *Educating Citizens;* Richard H. Hersh and Carol Geary Schneider, "Fostering Personal and Social Responsibility on College and University Campuses," and Bill Puka, "Teaching Ethical Excellence," *Liberal Education* 91.3 (Summer–Fall 2005): 6-13 and 22-25, respectively.

126 Pascarella and Terenzini, *How College Affects Students,* 2:328-39.

127 Parker J. Palmer, "Community, Conflict, and Ways of Knowing," *Change* 19.5 (1987): 20–25, on 22.

129 Rhetoric and the hidden curriculum: Chickering and Reisser, *Education and Identity*, 271, following Benson R. Snyder, M.D., *The Hidden Curriculum* (New York: Knopf, 1971), which explores the deepest implications of this situation. See also Frank Newman, Lara Coutourier, and Jamie Scurry, "Higher Education Isn't Meeting the Public's Needs," *CHE*, October 15, 2004, B6–B8.

130 Dumbing down of colleges: Paul Trout, "Student Anti-Intellectualism and the Dumbing Down of the University," *Montana Professor* 7.2 (1997), http://mtprof.msun.edu/Spr1997/TROUT-ST.html.

130 Students as customers: For a comprehensive view of the university in the light of market economics, see Robert Zemsky, Gregory R. Wegner, and William F. Massy, *Remaking the American University: Market-Smart and Mission-Centered* (New Brunswick, NJ: Rutgers UP, 2006).

130 Rona Wilensky, "For Some High School Students, Going to College Isn't the Answer," *CHE*, April 27, 2007, B18–B19. For similarly realistic views of where students are, see James M. Lang, "The Myth of First-Year Enlightenment," *CHE*, February 1, 2008, C1, C4, in part reporting on Tim Clydesdale's *The First Year Out: Understanding American Teens after High School* (Chicago: U of Chicago P, 2007).

132 "making the top ten": See Michael Arnone, "The Wannabes," *CHE*, January 3, 2003, A18–A19.

132 Influence of wealth and power on boards and faculties: See Robert M. Diamond, "Why Colleges Are So Hard to Change," *IHE*, September 8, 2006.

132 Roger W. Bowen: The New Battle between Political and Academic Cultures," *CHE*, June 22, 2001, B1.

133 Bok, *Our Underachieving Colleges*, 323.

134 Increasing tuition: See the data of the Center for the Study of Educational Policy at Illinois State, as reported by *IHE*, February 28, 2008.

135 " 'blended' courses": While it may have limited application to reform of entire curricula, combining face-to-face and online experience in the complete redesigning of individual courses can make deep improvement in their teaching power and economy. See C. A. Twigg, "Improving Learning and Reducing Costs: New Models for Online Learning," *Educause Review* 38.5 (2003): 29–38.

135 Prestige and money: See James Engell and Anthony Dangerfield, "Saving Higher Education in the Age of Money," *Liberal Education* 93.3 (2007): 14–21, and their excellent book of the same name.

INDEX

Coleman, Elizabeth, 79, 82, 155
Colgate University, 67
collaborative learning, 10
college education: defects of, 23; goals of, 10
Collegiate Learning Assessment Project, 55, 151
Collegiate Seminar Program (Strawberry Creek College), 18–35, 146–47; courses, 21–23, 33; evaluations of, 27–28, 29–32; individual major, 28–29
complexity of study, 40–42
Concordia College, 67
core curricula, 65–67, 153
Council of Graduate Schools, 157
courses: lecture, 6, 7; survey, 6, 7
Coutourier, Lara, 143
credit, academic, 49
critical thinking, 10
Crosstalk, 144
curriculum: hidden, 129; typical, 5. See also core curricula; new curriculum; "nuclear" curriculum

Dangerfield, Anthony, 4, 143, 144, 159
Dartmouth College, 67
Davidson College, 71
Davis, James R., 148–49
DEEP project, 94, 155
departments: academic, 18–19, 110; graduate, 118–19
depth, study in, 40, 148
Dewey, John, 17, 110, 156
Diamond, Robert M., 159
disciplines, basic, 39
dissertation, 114–16
distance learning and online education, 47–48
Dreyfus, Hubert L., 149
Duke Center for Academic Integrity, 51, 150

Educational Testing Service, 151
Education Trust, 158

Edwards, Alan F., Jr., 153
Edwards, Richard, 147
Ehrlich, Thomas, 150
Emerson, Diane M., 156
Emory University, 146
Empire State College, 85–87, 155
Engell, James, 4, 143, 144, 159
engineering education, 17, 145–46
England, James, 152
environmental education, 78, 154
ethical instruction, 126
Ettlich, Ernest E., 155–56
Evans, Daniel J., 88
Evergreen State College, 13, 87–96, 153, 155–56; courses, 90–92, 137–42

facilitation of meetings, 25
faculty, 36, 97–98; appointment and retention, 92–94; collegiality of, 27; responsibility of, 36–42; role of, in new curriculum, 52–53; –student ratio, 56
Fairhaven College, Western Washington University, 75–77, 154
Fallows, James, 151
Finkel, Donald L., 13–17, 145
Fish, Stanley, 126, 158
Fund for the Improvement of Post-Secondary Education, 20

Gaff, Jerry G., 148, 150
Gallatin School. See New York University
Gamson, Zelda, 148
general education curriculum, 65. See also core curricula
George Mason University, 67, 153
Germano, William, 157
Giroux, Henry A., 144
Glassick, Charles E., 152
Glazer, Judith S., 156
grading, 46; inflation of, 51, 150
graduate education, 112–19
graduate student assistants, 7–8, 21; exploitation of, 8, 113–14
Graham, Amy, 151